THE DOCTOR WHO PROGRAMME GUIDE

Volume 1

To my wife, Randy

THE DOCTOR WHO PROGRAMME GUIDE

Volume 1

Jean-Marc Lofficier

A TARGET BOOK

published by

the Paperback Division of

W.H. ALLEN & CO. PLC

A Target Book
Published in 1981
By the Paperback Division of
W. H. Allen & Co. PLC
44 Hill Street, London W1X 8LB

Reprinted 1983
Reprinted 1984 (three times)

Typeset by Phoenix Photosetting, Chatham
Printed and bound in Great Britain by
Anchor Brendon Ltd, Tiptree, Essex

ISBN 0 426 20139 6

ACKNOWLEDGEMENTS

I am deeply grateful to the following people who helped
me in the compilation of the information included in this
book: Jeremy Bentham, Christopher H. Bidmead, Eric
Hoffman, David Howe, Barry Letts, Ian Levine, John
McElroy, John Nathan-Turner, John Peel, Graham Williams, the BBC *Doctor Who* Production Office and the
Members of the *Doctor Who* Appreciation Society.

Special thanks are particularly due to Terrance Dicks,
whose help and advice were invaluable in the making of
this book.

J.-M.L.

This book gives details of *Doctor Who* programmes
televised by the BBC up to the time of going to press.

CONTENTS

FOREWORD

When a BBC Producer is a 142 years old (or does it just feel like that?), he regenerates and turns into an Executive Producer, or so they say; and then people from all over the world write and ask him questions; and he gets the answers wrong . . .

Well, perhaps I don't get them all wrong, but to be corrected by a 15-year-old about the third monster on the left in a show made before he was born can be an earth-shaking experience.

But now, thanks to the quite extraordinary industry of Jean-Marc Lofficier, I can be right every time. And so can you—and you—and you. Though you, sir, who pointed out that in various *Doctor Who* stories there have been three entirely different and incompatible versions of the destruction of Atlantis, presumably won't need the help of Jean-Marc.

Of course, he hasn't been able to put everything down; his self-imposed brief couldn't allow it even if he could have persuaded the publishers to accept a manuscript the length of the *Encyclopaedia Britannica*. In any case, a lot of it's secret.

For example, it will always remain untold that one of the monsters in an early Jon Pertwee story was familiarly known to one and all as Puff the Magic Dragon, looking as he did like an 8-foot-long pink-quilted pyjama case.

My lips will be even more firmly sealed about the various suggestions put forward concerning the interpersonal relationships of Alpha Centauri, the hermaphrodite hexapod. After all, even snails must have a surprisingly interesting social life and they don't have six arms.

Anything short of such revelations (which will only be made known 300 years after the Doctor's last regeneration) is sure to be found in this remarkable work of eccentric but dedicated scholarship.

Barry Letts

TABLE OF STORIES

The title of each serial is preceded by its story production code.

First Doctor (1963–1966)

First Season

A   An Unearthly Child (4 episodes)
(Episodes 2, 3 and 4 are also collectively known as The Tribe of Gum, but An Unearthly Child is the correct BBC designation for all four episodes.)

B   The Daleks (7 episodes)

C   The Edge of Destruction (2 episodes)
(Often wrongly referred to as Beyond the Sun)

D   Marco Polo (7 episodes)

E   The Keys of Marinus (6 episodes)

F   The Aztecs (6 episodes)

G   The Sensorites (6 episodes)

H   The Reign of Terror (6 episodes)

Second Season

J   Planet of Giants (3 episodes)

K   The Dalek Invasion of Earth (6 episodes)

L   The Rescue (2 episodes)

M   The Romans (4 episodes)

N   The Web Planet (6 episodes)

P   The Crusade (4 episodes)

Q   The Space Museum (4 episodes)

R   The Chase (6 episodes)

S   The Time Meddler (4 episodes)

Third Season

T   Galaxy Four (4 episodes)

T/A   Mission to the Unknown (1 episode)

U   The Myth Makers (4 episodes)

V   The Dalek Masterplan (12 episodes)

W   The Massacre (4 episodes)

Y   The Ark (4 episodes)

X   The Celestial Toymaker (4 episodes)

Z   The Gunfighters (4 episodes)

AA   The Savages (4 episodes)

BB   The War Machines (4 episodes)

Fourth Season

CC   The Smugglers (4 episodes)
DD   The Tenth Planet (4 episodes)

Second Doctor (1966–1969)

Fourth Season (continued)

EE   The Power of the Daleks (6 episodes)
FF   The Highlanders (4 episodes)
GG   The Underwater Menace (4 episodes)
HH   The Moonbase (4 episodes)
JJ   The Macra Terror (4 episodes)
KK   The Faceless Ones (6 episodes)
LL   The Evil of the Daleks (7 episodes)

Fifth Season

MM   The Tomb of the Cybermen (4 episodes)
NN   The Abominable Snowmen (6 episodes)
OO   The Ice Warriors (6 episodes)
PP   The Enemy of the World (6 episodes)
QQ   The Web of Fear (6 episodes)
RR   Fury from the Deep (6 episodes)
SS   The Wheel in Space (6 episodes)

Sixth Season

TT   The Dominators (5 episodes)
UU   The Mind Robber (5 episodes)
VV   The Invasion (8 episodes)
WW   The Krotons (4 episodes)
XX   The Seeds of Death (6 episodes)
YY   The Space Pirates (6 episodes)
ZZ   The War Games (10 episodes)

Third Doctor (1970–1974)

Seventh Season

AAA   Spearhead from Space (4 episodes)
BBB   The Silurians (7 episodes)
CCC   The Ambassadors of Death (7 episodes)
DDD   Inferno (7 episodes)

Eighth Season

EEE   Terror of the Autons (4 episodes)
FFF   The Mind of Evil (6 episodes)
GGG   The Claws of Axos (4 episodes)
HHH   Colony in Space (6 episodes)
JJJ   The Daemons (5 episodes)

Ninth Season

KKK   Day of the Daleks (4 episodes)
MMM   The Curse of Peladon (4 episodes)
LLL   The Sea Devils (6 episodes)
NNN   The Mutants (6 episodes)
OOO   The Time Monster (6 episodes)

Tenth Season

RRR   The Three Doctors (4 episodes)
PPP   Carnival of Monsters (4 episodes)
QQQ   Frontier in Space (6 episodes)
SSS   Planet of the Daleks (6 episodes)
TTT   The Green Death (6 episodes)

Eleventh Season

UUU   The Time Warrior (4 episodes)

WWW   Invasion of the Dinosaurs (6 episodes)
XXX   Death to the Daleks (4 episodes)
YYY   The Monster of Peladon (6 episodes)
ZZZ   Planet of the Spiders (6 episodes)

Fourth Doctor (1974–1981)

Twelfth Season

4A   Robot (4 episodes)
4C   The Ark in Space (4 episodes)
4B   The Sontaran Experiment (2 episodes)
4E   Genesis of the Daleks (6 episodes)
4D   Revenge of the Cybermen (4 episodes)

Thirteenth Season

4F   Terror of the Zygons (4 episodes)
4H   Planet of Evil (4 episodes)
4G   Pyramids of Mars (4 episodes)
4J   The Android Invasion (4 episodes)
4K   The Brain of Morbius (4 episodes)
4L   The Seeds of Doom (6 episodes)

Fourteenth Season

4M   The Masque of Mandragora (4 episodes)
4N   The Hand of Fear (4 episodes)
4P   The Deadly Assassin (4 episodes)
4Q   The Face of Evil (4 episodes)
4R   The Robots of Death (4 episodes)
4S   The Talons of Weng-Chiang (6 episodes)

Fifteenth Season

4V   Horror of Fang Rock (4 episodes)

4T	The Invisible Enemy (4 episodes)
4X	Image of the Fendahl (4 episodes)
4W	The Sunmakers (4 episodes)
4Y	Underworld (4 episodes)
4Z	The Invasion of Time (6 episodes)

Sixteenth Season

5A	The Ribos Operation (4 episodes)
5B	The Pirate Planet (4 episodes)
5C	The Stones of Blood (4 episodes)
5D	The Androids of Tara (4 episodes)
5E	The Power of Kroll (4 episodes)
5F	The Armageddon Factor (6 episodes)

Seventeenth Season

5J	Destiny of the Daleks (4 episodes)
5H	City of Death (4 episodes)
5G	The Creature from the Pit (4 episodes)
5K	Nightmare of Eden (4 episodes)
5L	The Horns of Nimon (4 episodes)
5M	Shada (6 episodes)

Eighteenth Season

5N	The Leisure Hive (4 episodes)
5Q	Meglos (4 episodes)
5R	Full Circle (4 episodes)
5P	State of Decay (4 episodes)
5S	Warriors' Gate (4 episodes)
5T	The Keeper of Traken (4 episodes)
5V	Logopolis (4 episodes)

FILMOGRAPHY

First Doctor

William Hartnell
1963–1966

First Season

Producers
Verity Lambert,
Mervyn Pinfield

Script Editor
David Whitaker

A   23 November 1963 to 14 December 1963
AN UNEARTHLY CHILD (4 episodes)
AN UNEARTHLY CHILD   THE FOREST OF FEAR
THE CAVE OF SKULLS   THE FIREMAKER

Writer
Anthony Coburn

Director
Waris Hussein

Regular cast: William Hartnell (the Doctor); William Russell (Ian Chesterton); Jacqueline Hill (Barbara Wright); Carole Ann Ford (Susan Foreman).

Cast: Derek Newark (Za); Alethea Charlton (Hur); Jeremy Young (Kal); Howard Lang (Horg); Eileen Way (Old Mother).

Story: Susan Foreman, 15, is the Doctor's granddaughter and goes to Coal Hill School, London. Two teachers, Ian Chesterton and Barbara Wright, go to investigate her home background. 'Home' appears to be a police box, which is in fact a TARDIS (Time and Relative Dimensions in Space), the Doctor's dimensionally transcendental spaceship, which plunges them all back to the Earth of 100,000 BC. They are captured by a tribe which has lost the secret of fire. Two leaders, Kal and Za, are involved in a power struggle. Ian makes a fire for Za by rubbing two sticks together, but Za does not allow the time-travellers to leave as promised. By a clever trick the Doctor and his companions escape to the TARDIS.

In this first story the Doctor is very much the anti-hero, and is portrayed as a tetchy, selfish old man.

B   21 December 1963 to 1 February 1964
THE DALEKS (7 episodes)

THE DEAD PLANET	THE EXPEDITION
THE SURVIVORS	THE ORDEAL
THE ESCAPE	THE RESCUE
THE AMBUSH	

Writer   *Director*
Terry Nation ·   Christopher Barry
Regular cast: see A above
Cast: Robert Jewell, Kevin Manser, Michael Summerton, Gerald Taylor, Peter Murphy (Daleks); Peter Hawkins, David Graham (Dalek voices); John Lee (Alydon); Philip Bond (Ganatus); Virginia Wetmerell (Dyoni); Alan Wheatley (Temmosus); Gerald Curtis (Elyon); Johnathan Crane (Kristas); Marcus Hammond (Antodus); Chris Browning, Katie Cashfield, Vez Delahunt, Kevin Glenny, Ruth Harrison, Lesley Hill, Steve Pokol, Jeanette Rossini, Eric Smith (Thals).
Story: The TARDIS, now stuck in the shape of a police box because of its faulty chameleon circuit, arrives on the planet Skaro inhabited by the blond Thals and the evil Daleks, both survivors of centuries of neutronic wars. After generations of mutation the Thals have become perfect human beings. The Daleks, who lost the use of arms, legs and bodies, are an evil intelligence housed in a protective metal casing. A Thal tells Susan that his race is starving. She asks the Daleks to help but they set a trap and the Thal leader, Temmosus, is killed. In a counterattack the Daleks—powered by static electricity from their

15

city floors—are defeated when the current is cut off, leaving them immobile.

This is the story which turned *Doctor Who* into an overnight success with over 8 million viewers.

Book: Doctor Who and the Daleks by David Whitaker
Film: Doctor Who and the Daleks

C   8 February 1964 to 15 February 1964
THE EDGE OF DESTRUCTION(2 episodes)

THE EDGE OF DESTRUCTION	THE BRINK OF DISASTER
Writer	*Directors*
David Whitaker	Richard Martin,
	Frank Cox

Regular cast: see A above
Cast: No others
Story: In a desperate attempt to gain control of the faulty TARDIS's guidance system and return the two school teachers to London 1963, the Doctor decides to experiment with a new combination. There is a violent explosion and the TARDIS blacks out. Susan and Barbara are convinced this is the work of an invisible alien force but Ian rationalises it as a technical fault. The irascible Doctor accuses the two teachers of sabotage; he suspects them of trying to blackmail him into returning them to Earth. Finally even Susan begins to suspect Ian and Barbara. However, they eventually realise that the halt has been caused by the ship's defence mechanism, which is also responsible for the psychological disturbances the crew are experiencing. The TARDIS has resorted to these measures because the Fast Return Switch jammed and the space ship was on its way back to the very beginning of Creation.

This is the only story which takes place entirely inside the TARDIS with no other cast than the regular actors.

D   22 February 1964 to 4 April 1964
MARCO POLO (7 episodes)

16

THE ROOF OF THE WORLD   RIDER FROM SHANG-TU
THE SINGING SANDS   MIGHTY KUBLAI KHAN
FIVE HUNDRED EYES   ASSASSIN AT PEKING
THE WALL OF LIES

Writer   *Director*
John Lucarotti   Waris Hussein

Regular cast: see A above

Cast: Mark Eden (Marco Polo); Derren Nesbitt (Tegana); Zienia Merton (Ping-Cho); Leslie Bates (the man at Lop); Jimmy Gardner (Chenchu); Charles Wadi (Malik); Philip Voss (Acomat); Philip Crest (Bandit); Paul Carson (Ling-Tau); Gabor Bareker (Wang-Lo); Tutte Lemkow (Kui-Ju); Peter Lawrence (Vizier); Martin Miller (Kublai Khan); Basil Tang (Foreman); Claire Davenport (Empress).

Story: The TARDIS lands in 1289 on the plateau of the Pamir. The time-travellers meet Marco Polo, a young Venetian emissary of Kublai Khan, who is on his way to Kublai's court in Peking, accompanied by a Tartar war lord named Tegana, a peace ambassador from the rival Mogul ruler, and a Chinese girl called Ping-Cho. Marco Polo forces the Doctor to join his caravan—he wants to present the TARDIS to Kublai Khan in the hope he will be allowed to return to Venice. But Tegana also wants the TARDIS and attempts to steal the ship; he tries to poison the party's water supply and drills holes in their water barrels as they cross the Gobi desert, then escapes on the last horse. Because of the intense night cold, condensation forms on the TARDIS so they survive. The party arrives in Peking; the Doctor meets Kublai Khan and they play backgammon. At first the Doctor wins 35 elephants, 4,000 horses and 25 tigers; then the tide turns and he gambles away the TARDIS. But when he exposes Tegana and saves Kublai's life the TARDIS's key is returned to him.

17

E   11 April 1964 to 16 May 1964
THE KEYS OF MARINUS (6 episodes)

THE SEA OF DEATH	THE SNOWS OF TERROR
THE VELVET WEB	SENTENCE OF DEATH
THE SCREAMING JUNGLE	THE KEYS OF MARINUS

Writer	*Director*
Terry Nation	John Gorrie

Regular cast: see A above

Cast: George Coulouris (Arbitan); Martin Cort, Peter Stenson, Gordon Wales (Voords); Robin Philips (Altos), Katherine Schofield (Sabetha); Heron Carvie (voice of Morpho); Edmund Warwick (Darrius); Francis de Wolfe (Vasor); Micael Allaby (Larn); Alan James, Anthony Verner (Ice Soldiers); Henry Thomas (Tarron); Raf de la Torre (Senior Judge); Alan James (Judge); Fiona Walker (Kala); Martin Cort (Aydan), Donald Pickering (Eyesen); Stephen Dartnell (Yartek).

Story: The travellers land on an island on the planet Marinus, where the sand is glass and the sea is acid. The TARDIS is captured by Arbitan, Keeper of the Conscience of Marinus, a machine that controls the island absolutely fairly. But four of the five keys that make it function are lost. The Doctor and his companions go to some strange places in search of them: the futuristic city of Morphoton, a deserted jungle, an ice-bound wilderness, and the city of Millenius. On their return they find Arbitan dead, murdered by Yartek, leader of the Voords, who now control the island. Ian is forced to hand over the four hard-won keys, but one is a fake—which causes the machine to explode, blowing itself and the Voords to pieces and freeing the inhabitants of Marinus from its domination.

Book: Doctor Who and the Keys of Marinus by Philip Hinchcliffe

18

F   23 May 1964 to 13 June 1964
THE AZTECS (4 episodes)

THE TEMPLE OF EVIL	THE BRIDE OF SACRIFICE
THE WARRIORS OF DEATH	THE DAY OF DARKNESS

Writer   *Director*
John Lucarotti   John Crocket
Regular Cast: see A above
Cast: Keith Pyot (Autloc); John Ringham (Tlotoxl); Ian Cullen (Ixta); Margot van der Burgh (Cameca); Tom Booth (Victim); David Anderson (Captain); Walter Randall (Tanila); Andre Boulay (Perfect Victim).
Story: The TARDIS lands in 1430 inside the Tomb of Yetaxa, one-time High Priest of the Aztecs. When the Doctor and his companions leave the Tomb the door locks behind them. They meet Autloc, High Priest of Knowledge and Tlotoxl, High Priest of Sacrifice. Autloc hails Barbara as Yetaxa's reincarnation—she is wearing the Priest's bracelet, which she found in the tomb. Ian is appointed Chief of the Aztec Warriors and as a result finds himself in competition with the Chosen Leader, Ixta, who eventually plunges to his death from a pyramid in a fight with Ian. Susan is made a handmaiden but she causes a rumpus when she refuses the last wish of the Perfect Victim—marriage. The Doctor rests in luxury with the esteemed elders and, although this seems incongruous, flirts mildly with a beautiful elderly Aztec lady, Cameca. This, however, is to learn from her a way into the Tomb to retrieve the TARDIS. Barbara is declared a fake after she petitions against human sacrifices but the crew escape when the Doctor opens the Tomb door with an old-fashioned wheel-and-pulley.

G   20 June 1964 to 1 August 1964
THE SENSORITES (6 episodes)

STRANGERS IN SPACE	A RACE AGAINST DEATH
THE UNWILLING WARRIORS	KIDNAP
HIDDEN DANGER	

A DESPERATE VENTURE

Writer	Directors
Peter R. Newman	Mervyn Pinfield, Frank Cox (episodes 5 and 6)

Regular cast: see A above

Cast: Stephen Dartnell (John); Ilona Rodgers (Carol); Lorre Cossette (Captain Maitland); Ken Tyllsen, Joe Greig, Peter Glaze, Arthur Newall (Sensorites); Eric Francis, Bartlett Mullins (Elders); John Bailey (Commander); Martyn Huntley, Giles Phibbs (Survivors).

Story: The TARDIS lands on the deck of a gigantic spaceship from 28th-century Earth. Its Captain, Maitland, explains they are under the control of a race called the Sensorites, who live on Sense-Sphere planet. They are all physically identical, with huge, bald, bulb-shaped heads. Through telepathic communication with Susan, the Sensorites invite them down to Sense-Sphere for talks. They explain they know the spaceship has discovered the mineral molybdenum on their planet, and they are wary of being exploited. The Sensorites fear the Humans because many of them have died since another spaceship left. The Doctor discovers deadly nightshade in the city's water supply and tracks down the culprits to underground caves—three deranged spacemen left behind from the previous expedition. The Captain promises to say nothing of the Sensorites' existence.

H 8 August 1964 to 12 September 1964

THE REIGN OF TERROR (6 episodes)

A LAND OF FEAR	THE TYRANT OF FRANCE
GUESTS OF MADAME GUILLOTINE	A BARGAIN OF NECESSITY
A CHANGE OF IDENTITY	PRISONERS OF CONCIERGERIE

Writer	Director
Dennis Spooner	Henrick Hirsch

20

Regular cast: see A above

Cast: Peter Walker (Small Boy); Laidlaw Dalling (Rouvray); Neville Smith (d'Argenson); Robert Hunter (Sergeant); Ken Lawrence (Lieutenant); James Hall (Soldier); Howard Charlton (Judge); Jack Cunningham (Jailer); Jeffrey Wickham (Webster); Dallas Cavell (Overseer); Dennis Cleary (Peasant); James Cairncross (Lemaitre); Roy Herrick (Jean); Donald Morely (Renan); John Barrard (Shopkeeper); Caroline Hunt (Danielle); Edward Brayshaw (Colbert); Keith Anderson (Robespierre); Ronald Pickup (Physician); Terry Bale (Soldier); John Law (Barrass); Tony Wall (Bonaparte); Patrick Marley (Soldier).

Story: The TARDIS lands in a forest clearing. The travellers think it's England 1963 but they are in fact 20 kilometres from Paris during Robespierre's Reign of Terror. A farmhouse is sacked by Government troops; the Doctor is concussed and left for dead, the others are dragged off to prison. The Doctor mascarades as a citizen, while Ian gets involved in the counter-revolutionary plot of English master spy James Stirling.

Second Season

Producers
Verity Lambert,
Mervyn Pinfield

Script Editor
David Whitaker

J 31 October 1964 to 14 November 1964
PLANET OF GIANTS (3 episodes)
PLANET OF GIANTS CRISIS
DANGEROUS JOURNEY

Writer
Louis Marks

Directors
Mervyn Pinfield,
Douglas Camfield
(episode 3 only)

21

Regular cast: William Hartnell (the Doctor); William Russell (Ian Chesterton); Jacqueline Hill (Barbara Wright), Carole Ann Ford (Susan Foreman).

Cast: Alan Tilvern (Forester); Frank Crawshaw (Farrow); Reginald Barrat (Smithers), Rosemary Johnson (Hilda); Fred Ferris (Bert).

Story: The doors of the TARDIS open. All readings indicate complete normality—but the travellers are only one inch tall! A crooked manufacturer, Forester, intends to capitalise on a new insecticide, DN6, to be used to increase food production for starving nations. He realises, however, that eventually the product will destroy every living thing for its molecules are stable instead of ephemeral. A Government Inspector, Farrow, finds out but is murdered by Forester before he can reveal his discovery. The crime is witnessed by miniaturised Ian and Barbara. The Doctor, against almost insurmountable odds—they are vulnerable to such hazards as being washed down plug holes and tumbling into matchboxes—stops Forester from publishing his bogus report on the scheme, using a gas jet and a match to cause an explosion that goes off in the evil Forester's face.

K   21 November 1964 to 26 December 1964

THE DALEK INVASION OF EARTH (6 episodes)

WORLD'S END	THE END OF TOMORROW
THE DALEKS	THE WAKING ALLY
DAY OF RECKONING	FLASHPOINT

Writer	*Director*
Terry Nation	Richard Martin

Regular cast: see J above

Cast: Bernard Kay (Carl Tyler); Peter Fraser (David Campbell); Alan Judd (Dortmun); Martyn Bentley, Peter Badger (Robomen); Robert Aldous (Rebel); Robert Jewell, Gerald Taylor, Nick Evans, Kevin Man-

22

ser, Peter Murphy (Daleks); Peter Hawkins, David Graham (Dalek voices); Ann Davies (Jenny); Michael Goldie (Craddock); Michael Davis (Thomson); Richard McNeef (Baker); Graham Rigby (Larry Madison); Nicholas Smith (Wells); Nick Evans (Slyther); Patrick O'Connell (Ashton); Jean Conroy, Meriel Horson (Women).

Story: The scene is London in 2164. The Daleks have invaded Earth, making many thousands of inhabitants into Robomen—Human Dalek servants—by clamping metal control discs to their heads. Other Slaves have been shipped to Bedfordshire, where the Daleks have a vast mining complex; they have discovered a fissure in the Earth's inner shell, through which they aim to remove the planet's core and replace it with a magnetic power system, so they can pilot Earth anywhere in the Universe. The Doctor and Ian are captured by Robomen and taken to the Dalek Supreme, who tries to change the Doctor into a Roboman, strapping him to an operating table in the Robotiser Chamber of a Dalek flying saucer parked in Trafalgar Square. The rest of the TARDIS crew escape from London and head for the mining fields, where Ian confronts the Slyther, the Daleks' man-eating pet. Susan and a freedom-fighter named David Campbell manage to gain entry into the complex and destroy the Daleks' radio network. No longer under the Daleks' control, the Robomen and the Slaves are encouraged by the Doctor to rise against their inhuman masters. A bomb is detonated, which destroys the Daleks and their craft. Earth is now safe and Susan, who has fallen in love with David Campbell, decides to stay behind.

Book: Doctor Who and the Dalek Invasion of Earth by Terrance Dicks

Film: The Daleks: Invasion Earth 2150 AD

Script Editor
Dennis Spooner

L   2 January 1965 to 9 January 1965
THE RESCUE (2 episodes)

THE POWERFUL ENEMY	DESPERATE MEASURES
Writer	*Director*
David Whitaker	Christopher Barry

Regular cast: William Hartnell (the Doctor); William Russell (Ian Chesterton); Jacqueline Hill (Barbara Wright); and introducing Maureen O'Brien (Vicki).
Cast: Ray Barrett (Bennett/Koquilion); Tom Sheridan (Captain).
Story: The Doctor lands on the planet Dido in the year 2493. He finds a crashed spaceship from Earth with two survivors: a paralysed man named Bennett and a young girl, Vicki. Bennett tells the Doctor that the rest of the crew have been murdered by the locals and Vicki says a native named Koquilion is protecting them from the further wrath of the enraged Didonians. The Doctor is suspicious of these explanations and challenges Koquilion—to find that he is Bennett in disguise. Bennett confesses that he murdered all the spaceship crew and the friendly Didonians to conceal a murder he had previously committed on the spaceship. He had planned to take Vicki—she is unaware of his crimes—back to Earth to testify to his innocence. However, terrified by two Didonian survivors, Bennett plunges over a cliff to his death. The Doctor offers Vicki a chance to join his crew and she accepts.

M   16 January 1965 to 6 February 1965
THE ROMANS (4 episodes)

THE SLAVE-TRADERS	CONSPIRACY
ALL ROADS LEAD TO ROME	INFERNO

Writer	Director
Dennis Spooner	Christopher Barry

Regular cast: see L above

Cast: Derek Sydney (Sevcheria); Nicholas Evans (Didius); Dennis Edwards (Centurion); Margot Thomas (Stall-holder); Edward Kelsey (Slave-buyer); Bart Allison (Maximus Petulion); Barry Jackson (Ascaris); Peter Diamond (Delos); Michael Peake (Tavius); Dorothy-Rose Gribble (Woman Slave); Gerton Klauber (Galley Master); Earnest Jennings and John Caesar (Men in Market); Tony Cambden (Messenger); Derek Francis (Nero); Brian Proudfoot (Tigilinus); Ann Tirard (Locusta); Kay Patrick (Poppea).

Story: The TARDIS crew have been resting up in a villa outside Rome in the year AD 64, while its owner campaigns in the Gallic Wars. When Vicki and the Doctor visit Rome, Ian and Barbara are captured by slave-traders—Ian is sold as a galley slave and Barbara to the court of Nero. The Doctor is mistaken for Maximus Pettulion, celebrated musician and enemy of Nero, and is taken to the Emperor's palace; but it is quickly obvious that he cannot play a note of music. Ian escapes from the galley ship only to be sent to Rome as a gladiator, where he encounters Barbara. With his spectacle lens the Doctor sets fire to plans Nero has rejected for his perfect city—inspiring Nero to start the Great Fire of Rome, under cover of which the crew of the TARDIS escape back to the villa.

Producer
Verity Lambert

N   13 February 1965 to 20 March 1965
THE WEB PLANET (6 episodes)

THE WEB PLANET	ESCAPE TO DANGER
THE ZARBI	CRATER OF NEEDLES

Writer   *Director*
Bill Strutton   Richard Martin
Regular cast: see L above
Cast: Robert Jewell, Jack Pitt, Gerald Taylor, Hugh Lund, John Scott Martin, Kevin Manser (Zarbi); Roslyn de Winter (Vrestin); Arne Gordon (Hrostar); Arthur Blake (Hrhooda); Joylyon Booth (Prapilius); Jocelyn Birdsall (Hlynia); Martin Jarvis (Captain Hilio); Ian Thompson (Hetra); Barbara Joss (Nemini); Catherine Fleming (voice of the Animus).
Story: The TARDIS is drawn by an unknown force to the planet Vortis. While the Doctor and Ian are busy exploring, the force causes Barbara to leave the TARDIS. Eventually she is captured by ant-like creatures, the Zarbi, who are at war with the butterfly-like Menoptera. She is taken to a slave colony and the Zarbi drag the TARDIS to their Web headquarters. The Doctor and Ian follow the tracks and the Doctor talks to the Animus, an unseen force, about an invasion by the Menoptera to regain their planet. The invasion is a failure but the Doctor manages to obtain an isotope brought to Vortis during the attack. When the Doctor and Vicki are taken to the Animus, Barbara manages to use the isotope and destroys the Animus. The Menoptera return to Vortis while the Zarbi become mindless creatures.

Book: Doctor Who and the Zarbi by Bill Strutton

P   27 March 1965 to 17 April 1965
THE CRUSADES (4 episodes)

THE LION	THE WHEEL OF FORTUNE
THE KNIGHT OF JAFFA	THE WAR-LORDS

Writer   *Director*
David Whitaker   Douglas Camfield

Regular cast: see L above

Cast: John Flint (William des Preaux); Walter Randall (El Akir); Julian Glover (Richard the Lionheart); David Anderson (Reynier de Marun); Bruce Wightman (William de Tornebu); Reg Pritchard (Ben Daheer); Tony Caunter (Thatcher); Roger Avon (Saphadin); Bernard Kay (Saladdin); Derek Ware, Valentino Musetti, Anthony Colby (Saracen Warriors); Jean Marsj (Joanna); Robert Lankesheer (Chamberlain); Zahra Segal (Sheyrah), Gabor Baraker (Luigi Ferrigo); Chris Konyils, Raymond Novak (Saracen Guards); George Little (Haroun); Petra Markham (Safiya); John Bay (Earl of Leicester); Sandra Hampton (Maimuna); Viviane Sorrel (Fatima); Diane McKenzie (Hafya); Tutte Lemkow (Ibrahim); Billy Cornelius (Soldier).

Story: The scene is 12th-century Palestine. Saracens, led by Emir El Akir, wait to ambush King Richard the Lionheart. The Doctor manages to save Richard. The King plans for peace by arranging a marriage between Saladdin's brother, Saphadin, and his own sister, Joanna, but Joanna refuses. The Doctor and Vicki narrowly escape being burnt at the stake as sorcerers.

Book: Doctor Who and the Crusaders by David Whitaker

Q   24 April 1965 to 15 May 1965
THE SPACE MUSEUM (4 episodes)

THE SPACE MUSEUM	THE SEARCH
THE DIMENSIONS OF TIME	THE FINAL PHASE

Writer	*Director*
Glyn Jones	Mervyn Pinfield

Regular cast: see L above

Cast: Peter Sanders (Sita); Peter Craze (Dako); Richard Shaw (Lobos); Jeremy Bulloch (Tor); Salvin Stewart (Messenger); Peter Diamond (Technician); Ivor Salter (Commander); Billy Cornelius (Guard); Murphy Grumbar (Dalek); Peter Hawkins (Dalek voice).

Story: The planet Xeros has been made into a space museum by the warlike Moroks. Among samples of their historical conquests are familiar aliens like the Daleks, and the Doctor and his friends—who have become invisible—see their own replicas in the museum. They realise that the TARDIS has jumped across a time track and to avoid ending up as exhibits they must change this possible future. They learn of a revolution planned against the Moroks and the Doctor helps the Xerons to victory. But an old enemy makes a reappearance . . .

R   22 May 1965 to 26 June 1965

THE CHASE (6 episodes)

THE EXECUTIONERS	JOURNEY INTO TERROR
THE DEATH OF TIME	THE DEATH OF DOCTOR WHO
FLIGHT THROUGH ETERNITY	THE PLANET OF DECISION

Writer	*Director*
Terry Nation	Richard Martin

Regular cast: see L above, and introducing Peter Purves (Steven Taylor) in the last episode.
Cast: Robert Marsden (Abraham Lincoln); Hugh Walters (William Shakespeare); Roger Hammond (Roger Bacon); Vivienne Bennett (Queen Elizabeth I); Richard Coe (TV announcer); The Beatles (Themselves); Jack Pitt (Mire Beast); Gerald Taylor, Kevin Manser, Robert Jewell, John Scott Martin (Daleks); Peter Hawkins, David Graham (Dalek voices); Ian Thompson (Malsan); Hywel Bennett (Rynian); Al Raymond (Prondyn); Arne Gordon (Guide); Peter Purves (Morton Dill); Dennis Chinnery (Albert Richardson); David Blake Kelly (Captain Briggs); Patrick Carter (Bosun); Douglas Ditta (Willoughby); Jack Pitt (Steward); John Maxim (Frankenstein's Monster); Malcolm Rogers (Dracula); Roslyn de Winter (Grey Lady); Edmund Warwick (Robot Doctor); Murphy Grumbar, Jack Pitt, John Scott Martin, Ken

Tyllson (Mechanoids); David Graham (Mechanoid Voices); Derek Ware (Bus Conductor).
Story: The Doctor finds through his new Time/Space Visualiser—with which he can see scenes from any time he wishes—that the Daleks are after him in a time machine of their own design. The two crafts engage in a frantic chase through the Cosmos. After a brief encounter on the desert planet Aridius, the TARDIS lands on the Empire State Building, the *Marie Celeste* (whose crew is exterminated by the Daleks), a Gothic house with Dracula and Frankenstein's Monster (who turn out to be amusement-park robots), and finally on the Mechanoid planet, Mechanus. There the travellers are taken prisoner after the Doctor's victory over a robot built in his image by the Daleks. They meet Steven Taylor, the only survivor of a crashed spaceship. The Daleks and the Mechanoids fight and destroy each other, but the Dalek time machine survives intact. Ian and Barbara use it to get back to their own time. Steven stays with the Doctor and Vicki.

Script Editor
Donald Tosh

S   3 July 1965 to 24 July 1965
THE TIME MEDDLER (4 episodes)

| THE WATCHER | A BATTLE OF WITS |
| THE MEDDLING MONK | CHECKMATE |

| *Writer* | *Director* |
| Dennis Spooner | Douglas Camfield |

Regular cast: William Hartnell (the Doctor); Maureen O'Brien (Vicki); Peter Purves (Steven Taylor).
Cast: Peter Butterworth (Monk); Alethea Charlton (Edith); Peter Russel (Eldred); Michael Miller (Wulnoth); Michael Guest (Hunter); Norman Hartley (Ulf); Geoffrey Cheshire (Viking Leader); David Anderson (Sven); Ronald Rich (Gunnar).

Story: The TARDIS materialises on the rocky east coast of England in 1066. There they are puzzled to find a modern wristwatch and an old gramaphone. Their owner, the Monk, is another time-traveller from the same planet as the Doctor. He is planning to ensure Harold's victory at Hastings with atomic bazookas. It takes all the Doctor's cunning to stop the meddling Monk. Finally he removes the Monk's dimension controller, leaving his TARDIS stuck in 1066.

This is the first story in which another member of the Doctor's race appears, although they are not yet identified as Time Lords.

Third Season

Producer	*Script Editor*
Verity Lambert	Donald Tosh

T   11 September 1965 to 2 October 1965
GALAXY FOUR (4 episodes)

FOUR HUNDRED DAWNS	AIRLOCK
TRAP OF STEEL	THE EXPLODING PLANET

Writer	*Director*
William Emms	Derek Martinus

Regular cast: William Hartnell (the Doctor); Maureen O'Brien (Vicki); Peter Purves (Steven Taylor).
Cast: Stephanie Bidmead (Maaga); Marina Martin, Susanne Carroll, Lyn Ashley (Drahvins); Jimmy Kaye, Angelo Muscat, William Shearer, Pepi Poupee, Tommy Reynolds (Chumblies); Robert Cartland (voice of the Rill); Barry Jackson (Garvey).
Story: The Drahvins and the Rills crashlanded on a deserted planet in Galaxy Four. The planet is about to explode so the women-dominated Drahvins plan to escape in the spaceship belonging to the alien but peace-

loving Rills. The true evil nature of the Drahvins eventually becomes apparent to the Doctor, who helps the Rills escape in their spaceship, with the aid of power from the TARDIS. The Doctor manages to escape the vengeance of the Drahvins thanks to the self-sacrifice of one of the Rills' friendly robots, the Chumblies.

T/A   9 October 1965
MISSION TO THE UNKNOWN
Writer   *Director*
Terry Nation   Derek Martinus
Regular cast: None
Cast: Edward de Souza (Marc Cory); Robert Cartland (Malpha); Jeremy Young (Gordon Lowery); Robert Jewell, Kevin Manser, Gerald Taylor, John Scott Martin (Daleks); Peter Hawkins, David Graham (Dalek voices).
Story: The setting is the planet Kembel, whence information of mysterious happenings has reached the Space Special Security Service. Agent Marc Cory is despatched to investigate, but almost at once disaster strikes: his crew are cut down one by one by Vaaga plants which infest the planet. But what Cory discovers is of vital importance for Earth's future: the Daleks are present in force on Kembel and their intention is to unify alien races to wipe out humans. Cory is exterminated by the Daleks but a tape containing the information he gathered survives.

This is the only one-episode story of *Doctor Who*. It does not feature the Doctor or any other of the regular cast and serves merely as a teaser for story V.

Producer
John Wiles

U   16 October 1965 to 6 November 1965
THE MYTH MAKERS (4 episodes)

TEMPLE OF SECRETS   DEATH OF A SPY
SMALL PROPHET, QUICK RETURN HORSE OF DESTRUCTION

Writer   *Director*
Donald Cotton   Michael Leeston-Smith

Regular cast: see T above, and introducing Adrienne Hill
(Katarina) in the last episode.
Cast: Cavan Kendall (Achilles); Alan Haywood (Hec-
tor); Ivor Salter (Odysseus); Francis de Wolff
(Agamemnon); Jack Melford (Menelaus); Tutte Lemkow (Cyclops); Max Adrian (Priam); Barrie Ingham
(Paris); Frances White (Cassandra); Jan Luxton (Messenger); James Lyam (Troilus).
Story: On the plains outside a besieged Troy the Doctor
is hailed as Zeus and taken by Achilles to his camp. But a
fellow warrior, Odysseus, is sceptical as to his authentic-
ity and gives him two days to devise a plan to capture
Troy. Meanwhile, the TARDIS is seized by Paris and
Vicki is hailed as a prophetess and given the name Cres-
sida. She and Steven are thrown into jail and Vicki is
given two days to prove her supernatural powers. At the
Greek camp the Doctor decides his attack on Troy will be
with a huge wooden horse. They wheel it into the city
and the Greeks emerge from inside the horse, open the
gates and take the city. Katarina, rescued from the ruins
of Troy by Steven, elects to go with the Doctor. Vicki
falls in love with Troilus and stays behind with him.

V   13 November 1965 to 29 January 1966
THE DALEK MASTERPLAN (12 episodes)

THE NIGHTMARE BEGINS   COUNTERPLOT
DAY OF ARMAGEDDON   CORONAS OF THE SUN
DEVIL'S PLANET   THE FEAST OF STEVEN
THE TRAITORS   VOLCANO

Writer   *Director*
Terry Nation Douglas Camfield
Associate Writer
Dennis Spooner (episodes 6, 8–12)
Regular cast: see U above, and introducing Jean Marsh
(Sara).
Cast: Brian Cant (Kert Gantry); Nicholas Courtney (Bret
Vyon); Pamela Greer (Lizan); Philip Anthony (Roald);
Kevin Stoney (Mavic Chen); Michael Guest (Inter-
viewer); Julian Sherrier (Zephon); Roy Evans (Trantis);
Douglas Sheldon (Kirksen); Dallas Cavell (Bors); Geof-
frey Cheshire (Garge); Maurice Browning (Karlton);
Roger Avon (Daxtar); James Hall (Borkar); Bill Meilen
(Froyn); John Herrington (Rhynmal); Terence
Woodfield (Celation); Peter Butterworth (Monk); Roger
Brierly (Trevor); Bruce Wightman (Scott); Jeffrey Isaac
(Khephren); Derek Ware (Tuthmos); Walter Randall
(Hyksos), Brian Mosely (Malpha); Robert Jewell, Kevin
Manser, Gerald Taylor, John Scott Martin (Daleks);
Peter Hawkins, David Graham (Dalek voices).

Episode 7 is a Christmas story, falling in the middle of
the main plot, and features: Clifford Earl (Sergeant);
Norman Mitchell, Malcolm Rogers (Policemen); Ken-
neth Thornett (Inspector); Reg Pritchard (Man in mack-
intosh); Sheila Dunn (Blossom Lefavre); Leonard
Grahame (Darcy Tranton); Royston Tickner (Stein-
berger P. Green); Mark Ross (Ingmar Knopf); Conrad
Monk (Assistant Director); David James (Arab Sheik);
Paula Topham (Vamp); Robert Jewell (Clown); Albert
Barrington (Professor Webster); Buddy Windrush (Prop
Man); Steven Machin (Cameraman).
Story: Many months after the death of Cory (see story
T/A), the Doctor lands on Kembel and finds a new
expedition from Earth led by Space Security Agent Bret

Vyon. The Doctor finds Cory's tape and he and Vyon decide to warn Earth of the impending Dalek attack. The year is AD 4000 and Mavic Chen, Guardian of the Solar System, has just betrayed Earth by giving to the Daleks the taranium element which will enable them to power their supreme weapon: the Time Destructor. The Doctor and his friends steal the taranium element but are unable to alert Earth as Chen has them branded as traitors. In the course of their escape from the Daleks Katarina sacrifices herself to save the Doctor. Bret Vyon is killed by his sister Sara Kingdom, who subsequently finds out the truth and helps the Doctor. After a chase across the Universe the TARDIS lands on the volcanic planet Tigus, where the Doctor meets his old enemy the Meddling Monk, who betrays him to the Daleks. Back on Kembel the Doctor finally activates the Time Destructor, which puts a stop to the Dalek invasion—but Sara is killed.

This was the longest *Doctor Who* story ever. Nicholas Courtney, who plays Space Agent Bret Vyon, later appeared in a part for which he is better known, Brigadier Lethbridge-Stewart of UNIT.

W   5 February 1966 to 26 February 1966
THE MASSACRE (4 episodes)

WAR OF GOD	PRIEST OF DEATH
THE SEA BEGGAR	BELL OF DOOM
Writer	*Director*
John Lucarotti	Paddy Russell

Regular cast: William Hartnell (the Doctor); Peter Purves (Steven Taylor), and introducing Jackie Lane (Dodo Chaplet) in the last episode.
Cast: Eric Thompson (Gaston); David Weston (Nicholas); John Tillinger (Simon); Edwin Fenn (Landlord); Christopher Tranchell (Roger); Erik Chitty (Preslin); Annette Robertson (Anne); Clive Cazen (Captain); Reginald Jessup (Servant); William Hartnell (Abbot of Amboise); Andre Morell (Tavannes); Leonard Sachs

(Admiral de Coligny); Cynthia Etherington (Old Lady); Barry Justice (Charles IX); Joan Young (Catherine de Medici); Michael Bilton (Toligny); Norman Claridge (Priest); Roy Denton, Ernest Smith (Men); John Slavid (Officer); Jack Tarran, Leslie Bates (Guards).

Story: It is Paris, just before the St Bartholomew's Day Massacre in 1572, and the Catholic Queen Mother, Catherine de Medici, is planning to murder all French Protestants. The Doctor disappears while Steven meets some Huguenots from the Protestant Admiral de Coligny's household. They rescue a servant girl, Anne, who has overheard the planning of the massacre. Later the Catholic Abbot of Amboise arrives at the Admiral's house. He is the Doctor's double. Steven believes he is the Doctor and follows him and overhears the plan to kill de Coligny. The attempt fails and Tavannes blames the Abbot for this failure and orders his execution. The Doctor returns, and he and Steven escape Paris as the massacre begins. In the last four minutes the TARDIS stops in Wimbledon and picks a young passenger, Dodo Chaplet (this segment was written by Script Editor Donald Tosh).

Script Editor
Gerry Davis

Y   5 March 1966 to 26 March 1966
THE ARK (4 episodes)
THE STEEL SKY   THE RETURN
THE PLAGUE   THE BOMB

Writers   *Director*
Paul Erickson,   Michael Imison
Lesley Scott
Regular cast: see W above
Cast: Eric Elliott (Commander); Inigo Jackson (Zentos);

35

Roy Spencer (Manyak); Kate Newman (Mellium); Michael Sheard (Rhos); Ian Frost (Baccu); Edmund Coulter, Frank George, Ralph Corrigan (Monoids); Roy Skelton (Monoid voice); Stephanie Heesom, Paul Greenhalgh (Guardians); Terence Woodfield (Maharis); Terence Bayler (Yendon); Brian Wright (Dassuk); Eileen Helsby (Venussa); Richard Beale (Refusian voice); John Caesar (Monoid).

Story: The Earth is about to plunge into the Sun. All Earth life is on a huge Ark on a 700-year journey to a new planet, Refusis. Dodo has a cold, against which Steven, the Human Guardians of the Ark and the slave race called Monoids have no immunity. The Doctor eventually finds a cure, and the travellers take off. In Episodes 3 and 4 the TARDIS lands on the Ark 700 years later—at the end of the voyage to Refusis. As a result of another bout of the cold, the Monoids are strong and have made the Guardians their slaves. With the help of the invisible Refusians, the Doctor forces the Monoids and the Guardians to make peace and live together on Refusis.

Producer
Innes Lloyd

X   2 April 1966 to 23 April 1966
THE CELESTIAL TOYMAKER (4 episodes)

| THE CELESTIAL TOYROOM | THE DANCING FLOOR |
| THE HALL OF DOLLS | THE FINAL TEST |

| *Writer* | *Director* |
| Brian Hayles | Bill Selars |

Regular cast: see W above
Cast: Michael Gough (Toymaker); Campbell Singer and Carmen Silvera (Joe and Clara, the Clowns); Peter Stephens and Reg Levers (the Hearts Family); Breyl

36

Brabham, Ann Harrison and Delia Linden (the Dancing Dolls); Peter Stephens (Cyril).

Story: The TARDIS materialises in the domain of the Celestial Toymaker, an evil force who dominates a fantasy world. He is a happy-looking mandarin character dressed in a splendid bejewelled coat. He makes the TARDIS intangible to the travellers and invites them to play games with him. The Doctor has to play the complex Trilogic Game while Steven and Dodo are set a series of puzzles, which if they lose will render them subjects of the Toymaker. They play Blind Man's Bluff—and win. Then they meet the Hearts family and play a macabre game of Musical Chairs. After that, they find themselves trying to reach the end of a ballroom dodging dancing dolls. Their fourth opponent is the obnoxious schoolboy, Cyril. With him, they play a death-trap dice game across electrified triangles, but manage to reach 'home' first. The Doctor triumphs over the Toymaker by imitating the magician's voice—and the travellers are on their way once again.

Z   30 April 1966 to 21 May 1966
THE GUNFIGHTERS (4 episodes)
A HOLIDAY FOR THE DOCTOR   JOHNNY RINGO
DON'T SHOOT THE PIANIST   THE OK CORRAL

Writer   *Director*
Donald Cotton   Rex Tucker
Regular cast: see W above
Cast: William Hurndell (Ike Clanton); Maurice Good (Phineas Clanton); David Cole (Billy Clanton); Sheena Marshe (Kate); Shane Rimmer (Seth Harper); David Graham (Charlie); John Alderson (Wyatt Earp); Anthony Jacobs (Doc Holliday); Richard Beale (Bat Masterson); Reed de Rouen (Pa Clanton); Laurence Payne (Johnny Ringo); Martyn Huntley (Warren Earp); Victor Carin (Virgil Earp).

Story: The Doctor, Steven and Dodo arrive in Tombstone on 26 October 1881. The Doctor has toothache and finds the local dentist is none other than the infamous gunslinger, Doc Holliday, who is feuding with the Clanton family. The Clantons' gunfighter, Harper, nearly shoots the Doctor by mistake. Marshal Wyatt Earp arrests the Doctor and rescues Steven from lynching. Pa Clanton hires gunfighter Johnny Ringo, but Earp wins the famous shoot-out at the OK corral.

AA   28 May 1966 to 18 June 1966
THE SAVAGES (4 episodes)

Writer	*Director*
Ian Stuart Black	Christopher Barry

Regular cast: see W above
Cast: Ewen Solon (Chal); Patrick Godfrey (Tor); Peter Thomas (Edal); Geoffrey Frederick (Exorse); Frederick Jaeger (Jano); Robert Sidaway (Avon); Kay Patrick (Flower); Clare Jenkins (Nanina); Norman Henry (Senta); Edward Caddick (Wylda); Andrew Lodge, Christopher Debham, Tony Holland (Assistants); John Dillon (Savage); Tim Goodman (Guard).
Story: On a distant planet live the ultra-civilised Elders and the wild primitive Savages. The TARDIS crew are escorted to the Elders' capital to meet Jano, leader of the City. Steven and Dodo are taken on a conducted tour. Inevitably the curious Dodo takes a detour, and finds herself in a strange laboratory presided over by Senta. When Dodo is back with the Doctor the truth suddenly dawns: the Elders' advanced civilisation has been formed by transferring the life force and energy of the Savages to the Elders. The Doctor finds this hard to believe but then his own life force is transferred to Jano. This means that Jano adopts some of the Doctor's attitudes—and conscience. With a new sense of justice Jano goes out into the Savages' wilderness and recruits them to destroy the transference laboratory. The Elders and the Savages

38

choose Steven to be their leader; Dodo and the Doctor
leave him to his task.

BB   25 June 1966 to 16 July 1966
THE WAR MACHINES (4 episodes)

Writer	*Director*
Ian Stuart Black	Michael Ferguson

Associate Writers
Kit Pedler,
Pat Dunlap
Regular cast: William Hartnell (the Doctor); Jackie Lane
(Dodo), and introducing Anneke Wills (Polly) and
Michael Craze (Ben Jackson).
Cast: Alan Curtis (Major Green); John Karvey (Profes-
sor Brett); Sandra Bryant (Kitty); Ewan Proctor (Flash);
William Mervyn (Sir Charles Summer); John Cater (Pro-
fessor Krimpton); Ric Felgate (Journalist); John Doye
(Interviewer); Desmond Cullum-Jones (Tramp); Roy
Godfrey (Taximan); Gerald Taylor (War Machine
Operator); John Rolfe (Captain); John Boyd-Brent
(Sergeant); Frank Jarvis (Corporal); Robin Dawson
(Soldier); Kenneth Kendall (Himself); George Cross
(Minister); Edward Colliver (Mechanic); John Slavid
(Man in phone box); Dwight Whylie (Announcer); Carl
Conway (Correspondent).
Story: In London's Post Office Tower the travellers find
Professor Brett and his revolutionary computer called
WOTAN—Will Opeating Thought Analogue device—a
universal problem-solver that can think for itself. Sud-
denly the machine reverses its process and starts to take
over men, beginning with Brett. WOTAN programmes
them to build War Machines, self-contained mobile
computers, to prepare for the takeover of Earth. Ben, a
young merchant seaman who has befriended Dodo, and
Brett's secretary, Polly, are captured, but Ben escapes
and warns civil servant Sir Charles Summer. Troops are
powerless against the War Machines but by using a series

of magnetic force fields the Doctor captures one and reprogrammes it to destroy WOTAN. Dodo decides to stay in England but Ben and Polly accompany the Doctor in the TARDIS . . .

This was the first modern-day story.

Fourth Season

Producer
Innes Lloyd

Script Editor
Gerry Davis

CC   10 September 1966 to 1 October 1966
THE SMUGGLERS (4 episodes)
Writer
Brian Hayles

Director
Julia Smith

Regular cast: William Hartnell (the Doctor); Anneke Wills (Polly); Michael Craze (Ben Jackson).
Cast: Terence de Marney (Churchwarden); George Cooper (Cherub); David Blake Kelly (Jacob Kewper); Mike Lucas (Tom); Paul Whitsun-Jones (Squire); Derek Ware (Spaniard); Michael Godfrey (Pike); Elroy Josephs (Jamaica); John Ringham (Blake); Jack Bligh (Gaptooth).
Story: The TARDIS materialises on a wild and remote part of 17th-century Cornish coast. Pirates are searching for treasure, while smugglers (who include the local squire) are trying to sell contraband. The Doctor unwittingly receives a clue to the treasure's whereabouts from the churchwarden—just before a pirate murders him. The pirates try to extract the information from the TARDIS crew, who are rescued by the militia.

DD   8 October 1966 to 29 October 1966
THE TENTH PLANET (4 episodes)
Writer
Kit Pedler

Director
Derek Martinus

Associate Writer
Gerry Davis (episodes 3 and 4)
Regular cast: see CC above
Cast: Robert Beatty (Gal Cutler); Dudley Jones (Dyson); David Dodimead (Barclay); Alan White (Schultz); Earl Cameron (Williams); Shane Shelton (Tito); John Brandon (Sergeant); Steve Plytas (Wigner); Christopher Matthews (Radar technician); Reg Whitehead (Krail); Harry Brooks (Jalon); Greg Palmer (Shav); Ellen Cullen (Technician); Glen Beck (Announcer); Callen Angelo (Cutler); Christopher Dunham (R/T Technician); Harry Brooks (Krang); Reg Whitehead (Jarl); Greg Palmer (Gern); Peter Hawkins, Roy Skelton (Cyberman voices).
Story: In the late 1980s the TARDIS lands at a South Pole Space Tracking Station, where General Cutler battles with invaders from the Tenth Planet, Mondas—Earth's missing half—which is draining away Earth's energy. The planet's inhabitants, called Cybermen, are ruthless and logical; their original bodies have been replaced with plastic to make them invulnerable and immune to disease. The Cybermen take control of Earth; they plan to use the powerful Z-Bomb at the South Pole base to destroy Earth before it destroys Mondas. They want to take Earth people to Mondas to turn them into Cybermen. Ben outwits them and before the Cybermen can again infiltrate the base Mondas absorbs too much energy and is destroyed. Without energy from Mondas to sustain them the Cybermen die. Worn out by the strain of recent events the Doctor seems to grow very old and when he returns to the TARDIS he begins to change . . .
Book: Doctor Who and the Tenth Planet by Gerry Davis

Second Doctor

Patrick Troughton
1966–1969

Fourth Season (*continued*)

Producer
Innes Lloyd

Script Editor
Gerry Davis

EE   5 November 1966 to 10 December 1966
THE POWER OF THE DALEKS (6 episodes)
Writer   *Director*
David Whitaker   Christopher Barry
Regular cast: Patrick Troughton (the Doctor); Anneke
Wills (Polly); Michael Craze (Ben Jackson).
Cast: Martin King (Examiner); Nicholas Hawtrey
(Quinn); Bernard Archard (Bragen); Robert James (Les-
terson); Pamela Ann Davy (Hensell); Edward Kelsey
(Resur); Richard Kane (Valmar); Peter Phorbes-
Robertson (Guard); Steven Scott (Kebble); Robert Rus-
sell, Robert Cuckham (Guards); Gerald Taylor, Kevin
Manser, Robert Jewell, John Scott Martin (Daleks);
Peter Hawkins (Dalek voice).
Story: The Doctor makes a complete recovery; a new
personality seems to inhabit his totally new physical
form. The TARDIS materialises on the Earth colony
Vulcan in the distant future. In a space rocket rescued
from the Mercury Swamp the Doctor fineds two inani-
mate Daleks. Lesterson, Chief Scientist of the colony,
has removed one, reactivated it, and plans to use the
Daleks as servants, but rebels trying to overthrow the
colony's Governor decide to use them for their own ends.

In fact the colony has already been infiltrated by Daleks, who have secretly set up a reproduction plant—on a conveyor-belt system—and plan to exterminate all Humans. But the Doctor finds their power source and turns it against them.

FF   17 December 1966 to 7 January 1967

THE HIGHLANDERS (4 episodes)

Writers	*Director*
Gerry Davis,	Hugh David
Elwyn Jones	

Regular cast: see EE above, and introducing Frazer Hines (Jamie).

Cast: William Dysart (Alexander); Donald Bisset (Laird); Hannah Gordon (Kirsty); Michael Elwyn (Ffinch); Peter Welch (Sergeant); David Garth (Grey); Sydney Arnold (Perkins); Tom Bowman (Sentry); Dallas Cavell (Trask); Barbara Bruce (Mollie); Andrew Downie (MacKay); Peter Diamond (Sailor); Guy Middleton (Attwood).

Story: The TARDIS lands on a Scottish moor in 1746 near the battlefield of Culloden, which has just seen the English defeat of the Scots and Bonnie Prince Charlie. The Doctor and his friends come across a group of hunted Highlanders led by clan laird Colin McLaren, accompanied by his daughter Kirsty and faithful piper Jamie McCrimmon. The Highlanders and the time-travellers are captured by English Lieutenant Algernon Ffinch. At the English camp a crooked solicitor named Grey is working on a scheme to transport prisoners to slavery in the West Indies. The Doctor escapes and gets arms to the Scottish prisoners, who are being held aboard a stolen ship. Grey and the Captain are overpowered and the ship returned to its owner, who takes the Scots to safety in France. The TARDIS dematerialises with an extra passenger—Jamie!

This was the last of the purely historical *Doctor Who* stories.

GG   14 January 1967 to 4 February 1967
THE UNDERWATER MENACE (4 episodes)
Writer   *Director*
Geoffrey Orme   Julia Smith
Regular cast: see FF above
Cast: Joseph Furst (Professor Zaroff); Catherine Howe
(Ara); Tom Watson (Ramo); Peter Stephens (Lolem);
Colin Jeavons (Damon); Gerald Taylor (Damon's Assistant); Graham Ashley (Overseer); Tony Handy (Guard);
Paul Anil (Jacko); P. G. Stephens (Sean); Noel Johnson
(Thous); Roma Woodnutt (Nola).
Story: The TARDIS lands on an extinct volcanic rock
surrounded by sea. On leaving the ship the Doctor and
his companions are kidnapped by the primitive Atlanteans and taken below the sea to the city of Atlantis.
There its inhabitants plan to sacrifice the travellers to
their Goddess Amdo, by suspending them over a pool of
hungry sharks. They are rescued by the scientist Zaroff,
who has a plan to destroy the world by draining the ocean
into its white hot core—so the super-heated steam will
explode the planet in two. Zaroff takes the Doctor with
him, sends Ben and Jamie to the mines, and orders that
Polly undergo an operation to become a fishworker,
collecting food from the sea. The TARDIS crew escape
and persuade the fishmen to revolt but Zaroff is unperturbed; he is confident that within 12 hours the world
will be destroyed. He becomes the victim of his own
scheme when the Doctor enters the generating plant and
accelerates the fission to break down the sea walls. Zaroff
is drowned by the flood waters; the others escape.

HH   11 February 1967 to 4 March 1967
THE MOONBASE (4 episodes)
Writer   *Director*
Kit Pedler   Morris Barry
Regular cast: see FF above
Cast: Patrick Barr (Hobson); Andre Maranne (Benoit);

44

Michael Wolf (Nils); John Rolde (Sam); Alan Rowe (Dr Evans; Space Control voice); Mark Heath (Ralph); Barry Ashton, Derek Calder, Arnold Chazen, Leon Maybank, Victor Pemberton, Edward Phillips, Ron Pinnell, Robin Scott, Alan Wells, Sonnie Willis (Crew); John Wills, Peter Greene, Reg Whitehead, Keith Goodman (Cybermen); Peter Hawkins (Cyberman voice); Dennis McCarthy (Controller Rinberg's voice).

Story: In the year 2070 Hobson and his deputy Benoit command a weather station on the Moon. There they operate the Gravitron, a gravity machine which has control over the weather on Earth. When the Doctor arrives he finds that a mysterious disease has broken out. He investigates and, to add to a number of other problems—like strange kidnappings and the Gravitron losing coordination—discovers that the Cybermen have landed. They are in fact responsible for the disease, and for the Gravitron's peculiar behaviour. They plan to take control of the kidnapped men and force them to operate the Gravitron to destroy Earth by drastically altering its weather. Polly fights back by spraying the Cybermen with plastic solvents but the main enemy force is rapidly approaching. Suddenly the Doctor realises that the Cybermen are susceptible to gravity variations—that is why they need humans to operate the Gravitron—so by deflecting the machine's action onto the Moon's surface he sends the Cybermen and their ships shooting off into distant Space.

Book: Doctor Who and the Cybermen by Gerry Davis

JJ   11 March 1967 to 1 April 1967
THE MACRA TERROR (4 episodes)
Writer   *Director*
Ian Stuart Black   John Davies
Regular cast: see FF above
Cast: Peter Jeffrey (Pilot); Graham Armitage (Barney); Ian Fairbairn (Questa); Jane Enshawe (Sunnaa); Sandra

Bryant (Chicki); Maureen Lane (Majorette); Terence Lodge (Medok); Gerton Klauber (Ola); Graham Leaman (Controller); Anthony Gardner (Alvis); Denis Goacher (Control voice); Richard Beale (Broadcast voice); Robert Jewell (Macra); John Harvey (Official); John Caesar, Steve Emerson, Danny Rae (Guards); Roger Jerome, Terry Wright, Ralph Carrigan (Cheerleaders).

Story The Doctor and his friends find themselves in the distant future on a planet run like a gigantic holiday camp. A man called Medok tells the Doctor it is being secretly infiltrated at night by a crab-like creature called Macra. The Macra are in fact in control of this 'paradise' and have conditioned the workers to quarry the deadly gas the Macra need to survive. The Doctor takes control of the gas-pumping machine and stops the Macra's vital supply. Ben clinches the victory and frees the colony by blowing up the gas pumps.

Producers
Innes Lloyd,
Peter Bryant

KK   8 April 1967 to 13 May 1967
THE FACELESS ONES (6 episodes)
Writers   *Director*
David Ellis,   Gerry Mill
Malcolm Hulke
Regular cast: see FF above
Cast: James Appleby (Policeman); Colin Gordon (Commandant); George Selway (Meadows); Wanda Ventham (Jean Rock); Victor Winding (Spencer); Peter Whitaker (Gascoigne); Donald Pickering (Blade); Christopher Tranchell (Jenkins); Madalena Nicol (Pinto); Bernard Kay (Crossland); Pauline Collins (Samantha Briggs); Gilly Fraser (Ann Davidson); Brijit Paul (Announcer);

Barry Wilsher (Heslington); Michael Ladkin (Pilot); Leonard Trolley (Reynolds).

Story: It is Gatwick Airport in 1966 and the TARDIS materialises on the runway in front of an incoming jet. While Polly hides in a hanger she is witness to the murder of a detective. Then Polly and Ben are kidnapped and the Doctor discovers others have disappeared—all passengers on Chameleon Tours charter flights. The kidnappers are the Chameleons, a race from another planet who have lost their identity in a nuclear explosion and are dying out. Their scientists have devised a method for taking over the identity of Humans, the transfer process taking four weeks. The Chameleons have lured onto aircraft and then miniaturised 50,000 passengers, now held on a space station hundreds of miles above the Earth. The Doctor succeeds in freeing them. Ben and Polly decide to remain in the England of 1966.

Script Editors: Gerry Davis and Peter Bryant

LL 20 May 1967 to 1 July 1967
THE EVIL OF THE DALEKS (7 episodes)
Writer   *Director*
David Whitaker   Derek Martinus
Regular cast: Patrick Troughton (the Doctor); Frazer Hines (Jamie); and introducing Deborah Watling (Victoria Waterfield).
Cast: Alec Ross (Bob Hall); Griffith Davies (Kennedy); John Bailley (Edward Waterfield); Geoffrey Colvile (Perry); Robert Jewell, Gerald Taylor, Murphy Grumbar, John Scott Martin (Daleks); Roy Skelton, Peter Hawkins (Dalek voices); Jo Rowbottom (Mollie Dawson); Marius Goring (Theodore Maxtible); Brijit Forsyth (Ruth Maxtible); Windsor Davies (Toby); Gary Watson (Terrall); Sonny Caldinez (Kemel).
Story: The TARDIS is stolen from Gatwick Airport and

driven off in a lorry. The Doctor and Jamie follow it to a Victoriana antique shop owned by Edward Waterfield. All three are transported back 100 years to the home of scientist Theodore Maxtible, who, with Waterfield's help, has devised a method of time-travel involving mirrors, static electricity—and the Daleks! The Daleks are holding Waterfield's daughter, Victoria, hostage so he is obliged to cooperate in their plan to bring the Doctor back to 1867. The Daleks want to acquire what they call 'the Human factor' to create an army of super-Daleks. They force the Doctor to run an experiment on Jamie registering every emotion he shows in his attempts to rescue Victoria. The plan backfires as they adopt attitudes of playful friendliness instead of Human cunning. All are recalled to Skaro where the Emperor Dalek now plans to inject the Doctor with the 'Dalek factor' which he will take back to Earth, and turn its inhabitants into Dalek-like creatures with the impulse to destroy. The Doctor is passed through a machine for transforming Humans into mental Daleks—but remains unaffected, for he is not Human. Instead, he manages to humanise some of the Daleks. Soon civil war erupts on Skaro between humanised Daleks and real Daleks. Maxtible, turned into a Dalek-like creature, is killed; Victoria's father saves the Doctor at the cost of his own life. The travellers depart whilst the war rages on . . .

Fifth Season

Producer　　　　　　　　*Script Editor*
Peter Bryant　　　　　　Victor Pemberton

MM   2 September 1967 to 23 September 1967
THE TOMB OF THE CYBERMEN (4 episodes)

Writers   *Director*
Kit Pedler,   Morris Barry
Gerry Davis

Regular Cast: Patrick Troughton (the Doctor); Frazer Hines (Jamie); Deborah Watling (Victoria Waterfield).

Cast: Roy Stewart (Toberman); Aubrey Richards (Profesor Parry); Cyril Shaps (Viner); Clive Merrison (Callum); Shirley Cooklin (Kaftan); George Roubicek (Hopper); George Pastell (Kleig); Alan Johns (Rogers); Bernard Holley (Haydon); Ray Grover (Crewman); Michael Kilgarrif, Hans Le Vries, Tony Harwood, John Hogan, Richard Kerley, Ronald Lee, Charles Pemberton, Kenneth Seeger, Reg Whitehead (Cybermen); Peter Hawkins (Cybermen voices).

Story: The TARDIS rematerialises in the future on the planet Telos where the time-travellers meet an Earth archaeological expedition financed by a strange couple named Kaftan and Klieg. They are excavating a tomb where the last Cybermen are rumoured to have been buried when their planet, Mondas, was destroyed. But the Cybermen are revived by a rise in the temperature engineered by the deranged Klieg. The party escapes from the tomb but the Cybermen retaliate by sending after them Cybermats—little metallic creatures trained to attack. The Doctor neutralises them and freezes the Cybermen to inactivity again.

Book: Doctor Who and the Tomb of the Cybermen by Gerry Davis

Producer   *Script Editor*
Innes Lloyd   Peter Bryant

NN   30 September 1967 to 4 November 1967
THE ABOMINABLE SNOWMEN (6 episodes)
Writers   *Director*
Mervyn Haisman,   Gerald Blake
HenryLincoln
Regular cast: see MM above

Cast: Jack Watling (Professor Travers); Norman Jones (Khrisong); David Spenser (Thonmi); David Grey (Rinchen); Raymond Llewellyn (Sapan); Charles Morgan (Songsten); Wolfe Morris (Padmasambhava); David Baron (Ralpachan); Reg Whitehead, Tony Harwood, Richard Kerley and John Hogan (Yeti).

Story: Explorer Travers is in the Himalayas searching for the Yeti when his companion is killed. Travers accuses the Doctor, whose TARDIS's rematerialised nearby, of his friend's murder. It appears, however, that the Yeti are fur-covered robots, directed by an evil Intelligence, a cosmic entity who now possesses the body of the Great Lama, an old friend of the Doctor. The Doctor finds a way to immobilise the Yeti and defeats the Great Intelligence. Travers finally discovers a real Yeti—a shy and harmless creature!

Book: Doctor Who and the Abominable Snowmen by Terrance Dicks

OO   11 November 1967 to 16 December 1967
THE ICE WARRIORS (6 episodes)

Writer	*Director*
Brian Hayles	Derek Martinus

Regular cast: see MM above

Cast: Wendy Gifford (Miss Garrett); Peter Barkworth (Clent); George Waring (Arden); Malcolm Taylor (Walters); Peter Diamond (Davis); Angus Lennie (Storr); Peter Sallis (Penley); Bernard Bresslay (Varga); Roy Skelton (Computer voice); Roger Jones (Zondal); Sonny Caldinez (Turoc); Tony Harwood (Rintan); Michael Attwell (Isbur).

Story: It is England during the Second Ice Age—AD 3000. The Doctor and his companions seek refuge in a scientific base where the ice barrier is being combatted with an ioniser. Embedded in the ice they find a perfectly preserved body: Varga, leader of the Ice Warriors, inhabitants of Mars who visited Earth during its first Ice

Age in prehistoric times. Revived, Varga captures Victoria and tries to force the Doctor to free the rest of his crew, still prisoners of the ice inside his spaceship. Learning that Varga plans to conquer the world, the Doctor manages to save Victoria and, taking over the base, uses the ioniser at full strength to create an explosion which melts the Ice Warriors and halts the ice flow.
Book: Doctor Who and the Ice Warriors by Brian Hayles

PP   23 December 1967 to 27 January 1968
THE ENEMY OF THE WORLD (6 episodes)

Writer	*Director*
David Whitaker	Barry Letts

Regular cast: see MM above
Cast: Henry Stamper (Anton); Rhys McConnochie (Rod); Simon Caine (Curly); Mary Peach (Astrid); Bill Kerr (Kent); Colin Douglas (Bruce); Milton Johns (Benik); George Pravda (Denes); David Nettheim (Fedorin); Patrick Troughton (Salamander); Carmen Munroe (Fariah); Gordon Faith (Guard Captain); Bill Lyons (Captain); Reg Lye (Griffin); Andrew Staines (Sergeant); Christopher Burgess (Swann); Adam Verney (Colin); Margaret Mickey (Mary); Dibbs Mather, Elliott Cairnes, Bob Anderson, William McGuirk (Guards).
Story: Arriving on an Australian beach, the time-travellers are attacked by an hovercraft, then rescued by an helicopter girl named Astrid. Her boss, Giles Kent, explains that the Doctor is the double of a would-be world dictator, Salamander. Jamie and Victoria infiltrate Salamander's retinue and discover he is the instigator of the 'natural' disasters sweeping the world. But they are captured and, to organise their rescue, the Doctor must impersonate Salamander. He penetrates the villain's HQ to be confronted by Kent, attempting to seize Salamander's power for himself. Salmander tries to impersonate the Doctor and steal the TARDIS—but he is ejected into space.

Producer   *Script Editor*
Peter Bryant   Derrick Sherwin

QQ   3 February 1968 to 9 March 1968
THE WEB OF FEAR (6 episodes)
Writers   *Director*
Mervyn Haisman,   Douglas Camfield
Henry Lincoln
Regular cast: see MM above
Guest star: Nicholas Courtney (Colonel Lethbridge-Stewart)
Cast: Jack Watling (Professor Travers); Tina Packer (Anne Travers); Frederick Schrecker (Julius Silverstein); Rod Beacham (Lane); Ralph Watson (Knight); Morgan Richardson (Blake); Jon Rollason (Chorley); Jack Woolgar (Arnold); Stephen Whittaker (Wems); Bernard G. High, Joseph O'Connell (Soldiers); John Levene, John Lord, Gordon Stothard, Colin Warman, Jeremy King, Roger Jacombs (Yeti); Derek Pollitt (Evans).
Story: The TARDIS is immobilised by a mysterious cobweb substance but the time-travellers escape and find themselves on a deserted London underground station. They meet an old friend, Professor Travers, who confesses he has reactivated a Yeti. This in turn has brought the return of the Great Intelligence. Yeti are at large in the underground, which is being invaded by the same cosmic cobweb which enveloped the TARDIS. The Doctor meets the man in charge of the Army's operations, Colonel Lethbridge-Stewart. Unfortunately, the Intelligence—through its mind control of the Colonel's Aide—captures the Doctor. A brain-draining helmet is placed on his head. But the Doctor has reversed the polarities and attempts to drain the Intelligence, and almost succeeds—until he is 'rescued' by his friends, leaving the Intelligence free again. After their departure Lethbridge-Stewart plans the creation of an interna-

tional task force to fight alien invasion.

This is a UNIT seed story.

Book: Doctor Who and the Web of Fear by Terrance Dicks

RR   16 March 1968 to 20 April 1968

FURY FROM THE DEEP (6 episodes)

Writer   *Director*

Victor Pemberton   Hugh David

Regular cast: see MM above

Cast: Victor Maddern (Robson); Roy Spencer (Harris); Graham Leaman (Price); Peter Ducrow (Guard); Jane Murphy (Maggie Harris); John Garvin (Curney); Hubert Rees (Chief Engineer); John Abineri (Van Lutyens); Richard Mayes (Baxter); Bill Burridge (Quill); John Gill (Oak); Margaret John (Megan Jones); Brian Cullingford (Perkins).

Story: The Doctor and his companions are suspected of sabotage at a North Sea gas refinery off the east coast of England. The refinery boss, Robson, blames them for the disappearance of rig crews, and leaks and pressure build-ups in the pipelines. The Doctor reports strange 'heartbeats' from the pipelines but Robson refuses to halt the gas flow. The noises come from a form of parasitic seaweed, which absorbs Human brains and transforms men into Weed creatures. The Weed launches an attack on the refinery, but after Victoria's screaming kills one, the Doctor realises that the creatures can be destroyed by high-frequency sound waves. After having killed all the creatures, the Doctor is ready to go on but Victoria decides to remain at the refinery.

SS   27 April 1968 to 1 June 1968

THE WHEEL IN SPACE (6 episodes)

Writer   *Director*

David Whitaker   Tristian de Vere Cole

(from a story by Kit Pedler)

Regular cast: Patrick Troughton (the Doctor); Frazer

Hines (Jamie), and introducing Wendy Padbury (Zoe). *Cast:* Deborah Watling (Victoria Waterfield— beginning of episode 1 only); Freddie Foote (Servo-Robot); Eric Flynn (Ryan); Anne Ridler (Dr Corwyn); Clare Jenkins (Tanya Lernov); Michael Turner (Bennett); Donald Sumpter (Enrico Casali); Kenneth Watson (Duggan); Michael Goldie (Laleham); Derrick Gilbert (Vallance); Kevork Malikyan (Rudkin); Peter Laird (Chang); James Mellor (Flannigan); Jerry Holmes, Gordon Stothard (Cybermen); Peter Hawkins, Roy Skelton (Cybermen voices).

Story: The TARDIS rematerialises inside a drifting rocket in which lurks a hostile Servo-Robot. The rocket itself is in the orbit of the Wheel in Space, a giant space station, where there have been reports of space rodents. The Doctor and Jamie are taken aboard the Wheel and find that the so-called rodents are Cybermats, a creation of the Cybermen, who are again planning an Earth invasion. With the help of a young programmer, Zoe, who joins the TARDIS crew, the Doctor succeeds in annihilating the Cybermen's invasion fleet, while the Wheel is attacked by a meteorite storm.

Sixth Season

Producer	*Script Editor*
Peter Bryant	Derrick Sherwin

TT   10 August 1968 to 7 September 1968
THE DOMINATORS (5 episodes)

Writer	*Director*
Norman Ashby	Morris Barry

Regular cast: Patrick Troughton (the Doctor); Frazer Hines (Jamie); Wendy Padbury (Zoe).

Cast: Ronald Allen (Rago); Kenneth Ives (Toba); Arthur Cox (Cully); Philip Voss (Wahed); Malcolm Terris (Etnin); Nicolette Pendrell (Tolata); Felicity Gibson (Kando); Giles Block (Teel); Johnson Bayly (Balan); Walter Fitzgerald (Senex); Ronald Mansell, John Cross (Council Members); Alan Gerrard (Bovem); Brian Cant (Tensa); John Hicks, Gary Smith, Freddie Wilson (Quarks); Sheila Grant (Quark voices).

Story: The TARDIS rematerialises on the planet Dulkis, now taken over by the alien Dominators and their deadly robot servants, the Quarks. The Dulcians are pacifists and cannot retaliate. They ignore the Doctor's warnings and some of them are captured. The Doctor discovers the Dominators' plan: to fire rockets down bore holes, causing an eruption of the molten core of the planet. They will then drop an atomic seed capsule down a bore hole, turning Dulkis into a radioactive mass, fuel for the Dominators' space fleet. Jamie and Cully, rebellious son of the Dulcian leader, become impatient and destroy a Quark. The Doctor and Zoe are captured by the Dominators. The Doctor intercepts the seed capsule as it is dropped and conceals it in the Dominators' flag ship, which is then destroyed in an atomic blast.

UU   14 September 1968 to 12 October 1968
THE MIND ROBBER (5 episodes)

Writer	*Director*
Peter Ling	David Maloney

Regular cast: see TT above

Cast: Emrys Jones (Master of the Land); John Atterbury, Ralph Carrigan, Bill Weisner, Terry Wright (White Robots); Hamish Wilson (Jamie); Philip Ryan (Redcoat); Bernard Horsfall (Gulliver); Barbara Loft, Sylvestra Tozel, Timothy Horton, Martin Langley, Christopher Reynolds, David Reynolds (Children); Paul Alexander, Ian Hines, Richard Ireson (Clockwork Soldiers); Christine Pirie (Rapunzel); Sue Pulford (Medusa);

Christopher Robbie (Karkus); David Cannon (Cyrano); John Greenwood (D'Artagnan and Lancelot); Gerry Wain (Blackbeard).

Story: To escape a lava flow the TARDIS jumps out of Space and Time, and arrives in the Land of Fiction, a huge white void where fiction appears as reality. The travellers are hunted by White Robots and encounter mechanical soldiers. Jamie gains entrance to the Citadel of the Master, an aged gentleman who wants to retire and insists that the Doctor takes his place. The Doctor refuses, so the White Robots capture Jamie and Zoe. In the following battle of wits the Doctor calls up champions from famous Earth fictions to defeat the Master. Meanwhile, Zoe finds the true Master of the Land: a giant computer. They manage to overload the machine and escape.

Script Editor
Terrance Dicks

VV   2 November 1968 to 21 December 1968
THE INVASION (8 episodes)
Writer   *Director*
Derrick Sherwin   Douglas Camfield
(from a story by Kit Pedler)
Regular cast: see TT above
Guest stars: Nicholas Courtney (Brigadier Lethbridge-Stewart); John Levene (Benton).
Cast: Murray Evans (Lorry Driver); Walter Randall (Patrolman); Sally Faulkner (Isobel Watkins); Geoffrey Cheshire (Tracy); Kevin Stoney (Tobias Vaughn); Peter Halliday (Packer); Edward Burnham (Professor Watkins); Ian Fairbairn (Gregory); James Thornhill (Sergeant Walters); Robert Sidaway (Captain Turner); Sheila Dunn (Operator); Edward Dentith (Rutlidge); Peter Thompson (Workman); Dominic Allan (Policeman); Stacy Davies (Perkins); Clifford Earl (Branwell);

Norman Hatley (Peters); Reg Whitehead, Greg Palmer, Pat Gorman, Harry Brooks, John Wills, Tony Harwood (Cybermen).

Story: The Doctor, back in 20th-century London, calls at the home of his friend Professor Travers, but finds that he has let it to a computer scientist, Professor Watkins, and his niece Isobel. Watkins has disappeared—last heard of at International Electromatics, a firm controlling all the world's computers. The Doctor visits the firm and distrusts the managing director, Tobias Vaughn. So does Brigadier Lethbridge-Stewart of the newly formed UNIT (United Nations Intelligence Taskforce). Zoe and Isobel are captured by Vaughn, who is forcing Watkins to develop the Cerebration Mentor, the purpose of which is to generate emotional impulses. The Doctor discovers Vaughn is in the power of the Cybermen—but too late. The Cybermen manage to paralyse Earth's population and launch an invasion through the sewers, in which their troops had been previously hidden by Vaughn's men. By firing a missile to the dark side of the Moon, where the paralysing weapon of the Cybermen is hidden, the Doctor manages to defeat the Cybermen and wipe out their invasion fleet. With the help of a now-reformed Vaughn he destroys the last Cyberman craft which was preparing to annihilate Earth with a megaton bomb.

This is the first UNIT story.

WW   28 December 1968 to 18 January 1969
THE KROTONS (4 episodes)
Writer   *Director*
Robert Holmes   David Maloney
Regular cast: see TT above
Cast: James Copeland (Selris); Gilbert Wynne (Thara); Terence Brown (Abu); Madeleine Mills (Vana); Philip Madoc (Eelek); Richard Ireson (Axus); James Cairncross (Beta); Maurice Selwyn (Custodian); Bronson Shaw (Student); Robert La Bassiere, Miles Northover

57

(Krotons); Roy Skelton, Patrick Tull (Kroton voices).
Story: The primitive Gonds are ruled and taught by means of the Kroton Machine. The Krotons are crystalline beings waiting in suspended animation until they have drained enough mental energy from the Gonds' brains to be reanimated. Each year the two most brilliant Gonds are lured into the Kroton Machine. Zoe and the Doctor take the Teaching Machine Test and their mental power reanimates the Krotons. The Doctor discovers the Kroton life system is based on telurium and destroys them with sulphuric acid.

XX   25 January 1969 to 1 March 1969
THE SEEDS OF DEATH (6 episodes)
Writer   *Director*
Brian Hayles   Michael Ferguson
Regular cast: see TT above
Cast: Alan Bennion (Slaar); Steve Peters (Ice Warrior); Philip Ray (Eldred); Louise Pajo (Gia Kelly); John Witty (Computer voice); Ric Felgate (Brent); Harry Towb (Osgood); Ronald Leigh-Hunt (Radnor); Terry Scully (Fewsham); Christopher Coll (Phipps); Martin Cort (Locke); Tony Harwood, Sonny Caldinez (Ice Warriors); Derrick Slater (Guard); Graham Leaman (Marshal); Hugh Morton (Sir James Gregson).
Story: Earth in the 21st century enjoys the T-Mat, a form of instantaneous travel directed from a Moon relay station. The machine breaks down and the Doctor investigates. He finds the Moon overrun by Ice Warriors, who are preparing to launch an invasion against Earth. To weaken Earth's resistance they are using the T-Mat to send Martian Seed Pods, which emit a lethal fungus, over Earth's winter zones. The Doctor manages to get himself and the T-Mat back to a chaotic Earth, where Ice Warriors have taken control of the weather. The Doctor finds that the only thing that can destroy the fungus is heavy rains and warmth, which he provokes after regain-

ing control of the weather station. A solar heat gun takes
care of the Ice Warriors.

Script Editor: Derrick Sherwin

YY   8 March 1969 to 12 April 1969
THE SPACE PIRATES (6 episodes)
Writer   *Director*
Robert Holmes   Michael Hart
Regular cast: see TT above
Cast: Brian Peck (Dervise); Dudley Foster (Caven); Jack
May (Hermack); Donald Gee (Warne); George Layton
(Penn); Nick Zaran (Sorba); Anthony Donovan
(Guard); Gordon Gostelow (Clancey); Lisa Daniely
(Madeleine); Steve Peters (Guard); Edmond Knight
(Dom Issigri).
Story: The TARDIS materialises on a navigation beacon
far out in space. A group of space pirates, using explo-
sives, breaks up the beacon into its constituent parts in
an attempt to steal it. The Doctor and his companions are
separated from the TARDIS, which is on a part of the
beacon the pirates manage to steal. The International
Space Corps is convinced that the thief is an innocent yet
eccentric space mining pioneer named Milo Clancey.
Milo joins forces with the Doctor, and the TARDIS crew
hide him on the planet Ta. Here dwells Caven, a notorious space criminal in league with space pirates, and
responsible for the theft. He is assisted by Madeleine,
daughter of his ex-partner Dom Issigri, who is now
Caven's captive. Madeleine sees the error of her ways and
Caven is arrested.

Producer   *Script Editor*
Derrick Sherwin   Terrance Dicks

ZZ   19 April 1969 to 21 June 1969
THE WAR GAMES (10 episodes)

Writers   *Director*
Malcolm Hulke,   David Maloney
Terrance Dicks

Regular cast: see TT above

Cast: Jane Sherwin (Lady Buckingham); David Savile
(Carstairs); John Livesby, Bernard Davies (German Sol-
diers); Terence Buyler (Barrington); Brian Forster (Wil-
lis); Noel Coleman (General Smythe); Hubert Rees
(Captain Ransome); Esmond Webb (Burns); Richard
Steele (Gorton); Peter Stanton (Chauffeur); Pat Gorman
(Policeman); Tony McEwan (Redcoat); David Valla
(Crane); Gregg Palmer (Lucke); David Garfield (Von
Weich); Edward Brayshaw (War Chief); Philip Madoc
(War Lord); James Bree (Security Chief); Bill Hutchin-
son (Thompson); Terry Adams (Riley); Leslie Schofield
(Leroy); Vernon Dubycheff (Scientist), Rudolph
Walker (Harper); John Atterbury, Charles Pemberton
(Aliens); Michael Lynch (Spencer); Graham Weston
(Russell); David Troughton (Moor); Peter Craze (Du
Pont); Michael Napier (Villar); Stephen Hubay (Pet-
rov); Bernard Horsfall, Trevor Martin, Clyde Pollitt
(Time Lords); Clare Jenkins (Tanya); Freddie Wilson
(Quark); John Levene (Yeti); Tony Harwood (Ice War-
rior); Roy Pearce (Cyberman); Robert Jewell (Dalek).

Story: The TARDIS materialises in what apears to be
no-man's-land on a First World War battlefront in
France. When the Doctor and his companions emerge
from a cloud of mist they find that they are really on
another planet. It is split into time zones and a fierce war
is being waged in each one. The wars are controlled by
aliens, who have gathered soldiers from many periods of
history, brainwashed them and put them to battle with
the aim of forming an invincible army from the survivors
to take over the Galaxy. The Doctor is identified by the
War Chief, assistant to the leader of the aliens, the War

Lord, but he manages to seize the alien HQ with the help of soldiers no longer under the aliens' control, and calls on the Time Lords for help.

The Time Lords are a nearly omnipotent race, with the ability to control Time and Space. Both the Doctor and the War Chief are renegade Time Lords who each stole a TARDIS and escaped. The Doctor fled to explore the Universe (Time Lord policy is one of strict non-intervention) whilst the War Chief gave Time Lord technology to the War Lords—in particular the SIDRATs, an inferior kind of TARDIS—which enabled him to start the war games. The Time Lords intervene, capture and execute the War Lord, return all the soldiers to their proper time zones on earth and, finally, try the Doctor. They find him guilty of intervention and exile him to Earth after having changed his appearance. Jamie and Zoe are returned to their respective eras.

This is the first story introducing the Time Lords—and explaining the Doctor's origins.
Book: Doctor Who and the War Games by Malcolm Hulke

Third Doctor

Jon Pertwee
1970–1974

Seventh Season

Producer
Derrick Sherwin

Script Editor
Terrance Dicks

AAA   3 January 1970 to 24 January 1970
SPEARHEAD FROM SPACE (4 episodes)
Writer   *Director*
Robert Holmes   Derek Martinus
Regular cast: Jon Pertwee (the Doctor), Caroline John
(Liz Shaw).
Guest star: Nicholas Courtney (Brigadier Lethbridge-
Stewart)
Cast: Hugh Burden (Channing); Neil Wilson (Seeley);
John Breslin (Captain Munro); Anthony Webb (Dr
Henderson); Helen Dorward (Nurse); Talfryn Thomas
(Mullins); George Lee (Captain Forbes); Iain Smith,
Tessa Shaw, Ellis Jones (UNIT men); Allan Mitchell
(Wagstaff); Prentis Hancock (Reporter); Derek Smee
(Ransome); John Woodnutt (Hibbert); Betty Bowden
(Meg Seeley); Hamilton Dyce (Scobie); Henry McCar-
thy (Dr Beavis); Clifford Cox (Soldier); Edmund Bailey
(Waxworks Attendant).
Story: A shower of meteorites falls on Essex and the
Brigadier and his newly recruited scientist Liz Shaw,
from Cambridge, enlist the aid of a physically changed
Doctor to investigate the phenomenon. Factory boss
Channing is a Nestene—a member of an alien collective

intelligence which colonises planets by copying native life forms. Nestenes have a special ability to control plastic; Channing is making Autons, plastic mannikins able to fight and kill, controlled by the Nestene Consciousness. He has also been making plastic facsimiles of Cabinet members to enable him to gain world domination. The Doctor manages to defeat the Nestene as the Autons start on a killing rampage. He agrees to work for UNIT as scientific advisor, in return for facilities to repair the TARDIS, grounded by the Time Lords on 20th-century Earth. The Brigadier gives him a sprightly yellow roadster—Bessie.
Book: Doctor Who and the Auton Invasion by Terrance Dicks

Producer
Barry Letts

BBB   31 January 1970 to 14 March 1970
THE SILURIANS (7 episodes)
Writer   *Director*
Malcolm Hulke   Timothy Combe
Regular cast: see AAA above
Guest star: see AAA above
Cast: John Newman (Spencer); Bill Matthews (Davis); Peter Miles (Dr Lawrence); Norman Jones (Baker); Thomasine Heiner (Miss Dawson); Fulton Mackay (Dr Quinn); Roy Braningan (Roberts); Ian Cunningham (Dr Meredith); Paul Barrow (Hawkins); Pat Gorman (Silurian Scientist); Dave Carter (Old Silurian); Nigel John (Young Silurian); Paul Barton, Simon Cain, John Churchill, Dave Carter (Silurians); Peter Halliday (Silurian voice); Nancie Jackson (Doris Squire); Gordon Richardson (Squire); Richard Steel (Hart); Ian Talbot (Travis); Geoffrey Palmer (Masters); Harry Swift (Robins); Brendan Barry (Doctor); Darek Pallitt

(Wright); Alan Mason (Corporal Nutting).

Story: On Wenley Moor, a secret Derbyshire atomic research centre where a reactor converting nuclear energy to electrical power is being developed, work is being held up by inexplicable power losses and breakdowns among staff. The Doctor traces the trouble to underground caves where prehistoric monsters live with a nest of highly intelligent man-like reptiles, the Silurians. They went into hibernation millions of years ago but have been resuscitated by accidental electric discharges from the research centre. They now claim back 'their' Earth. The Doctor strives for harmony between Man and Silurian and at first seems to succeed with the Old Silurian. But then the rebellious and intolerant Young Silurian releases a terrible disease that will wipe out the Universe. The Doctor finds an antidote. The Silurians take over the research centre and plan to destroy the Van Allen Belt, which shields Earth from the Sun. The reptiles are tricked into returning to their caves by the threat of radiation and the Brigadier—to the Doctor's disgust—blows them up.

Book: Doctor Who and the Cave Monsters by Malcolm Hulke

CCC   21 March 1970 to 2 May 1970
THE AMBASSADORS OF DEATH (7 episodes)
Writer   *Director*
David Whitaker   Michael Ferguson
Regular cast: see AAA above
Guest stars: see AAA above, and John Levene (Sergeant Benton).
Cast: Robert Cawdron (Taltalian); Ric Felgate (Van Lynden); Ronald Allen (Ralph Cornish); Michael Wisher (John Wakefield); Cheryl Molineaux (Miss Rutherford); John Abineri (Carrington); Ray Armstrong (Grey); Robert Robertson (Collinson); Ivan Moreno (Dobson); James Haswell (Champion); Bernard Martin

64

(Control Room Assistant); Dallas Cavell (Quinian); Steve Peters, Neville Simons (Astronauts); Gordon Sterne (Heldorf); William Dysart (Reegan); Cyril Shaps (Lennox); John Lord (Masters); Max Faulkner (Soldier); Joanna Ross (First Assistant); Carl Conway (Second Assistant); Ric Felgate (Astronaut); James Clayton (Parker); Peter Noel Cook (Alien); Peter Halliday (Alien voice); Neville Simons (Michaels); Steve Peters (Lefee); Geoffrey Reeves (Johnson).

Story: Seven months after leaving Mars the *Probe* 7 ship has still not returned to earth and a *Recovery* 7 rocket is despatched to investigate. *Recovery* 7 returns to Earth but, after landing, the astronauts are kidnapped by men masquerading as UNIT forces. Liz Shaw notices the ship's Geiger counter is at maximum; the crew would normally have been killed by radiation. The Doctor is convinced the crew are not Human. He makes a solo space mission and finds the real astronauts held aboard a large alien spaceship. The captain of the alien ship asks for the return of his 'ambassadors' or he will destroy the planet. The three recaptured aliens are exchanged.

DDD   9 May 1970 to 20 June 1970
INFERNO (7 episodes)
Writer   *Director*
Don Houghton   Douglas Camfield
Regular cast: see AAA above
Guest stars: see CCC above
Cast: Olaf Pooley (Stahlman); Christopher Benjamin (Sir Gold); Ian Fairbairn (Bromley); Walter Randall (Slocum); Sheila Dunn (Petra Williams); Derek Newark (Greg Sutton); David Simeon (Latimer); Derek Ware (Wyatt); Roy Scannell (Sentry); Keith James (Patterson); Dave Carter, Pat Gormon, Philip Ryan, Peter Thompson, Walter Henry (Primords).

Story: A crisis develops on a top-secret drilling project—Inferno—which aims to penetrate the Earth's crust and release a new energy source to be called Stahl-man's Gas, named after Professor Stahlman, in charge of Inferno. The drilling pipes are leaking a liquid which turns green on contact with Human skin and transforms its victims into vicious primeval ape-like creatures called Primords. The Doctor is transported by accident into a parallel world, where England is ruled by a military dictatorship and Inferno is about to destroy the planet. Thwarted by his friends' counterparts on this parallel world, the Doctor is powerless to stop the destruction of the planet but manages to escape and return to Earth. There, he overcomes the power-crazed Professor Stahl-man, who has become a Primord and threatens to unleash the full forces of Inferno.

Eighth Season

Producer	*Script Editor*
Barry Letts	Terrance Dicks

EEE   2 January 1971 to 23 January 1971
TERROR OF THE AUTONS (4 episodes)

Writer	*Director*
Robert Holmes	Barry Letts

Regular cast: Jon Pertwee (the Doctor); Katy Manning (Jo Grant).
Guest stars: Nicholas Courtney (Brigadier Lethbridge-Stewart); Roger Delgado (the Master); John Levene (Sergeant Benton); Richard Franklin (Captain Yates).
Cast: John Baskomb (Rossini); Dave Carter (Museum Attendant); Christopher Burgess (Professor Phillips); Andrew Staines (Goodge); Frank Mills (Radiotelescope Director); David Garth (Time Lord); Michael Wisher (Rex Farrel); Harry Towb (McDermott); Barbara Leake (Mrs Farrel); Stephen Jack (Farrel Sr); Roy Stewart (Strong Man); Terry Walsh, Pat Gorman (Autons);

Haydn Jones (Auton voice); Dermot Tuohy (Brown-rose); Norman Stanley (Telephone Man).
Story: The Master, another renegade Time Lord, materialises in a horsebox-like TARDIS at Rossini's Circus. Warned of his prescence by another Time Lord, the Doctor and his new assistant, Jo Grant, realise that, with the Master's help, the Nestenes are planning a new invasion, using the Autons. The Doctor thwarts all the plans of the Nestenes, including the lethal use, under Nestene control, of a plastic flower. The Master, to save his own life, helps the Doctor prevent the materialisation of the Nestene Monster. He then escapes to fight another day.

This is the first story in which the Master appears.
Book: Doctor Who and the Terror of the Autons by Terrance Dicks

FFF   30 January 1971 to 6 March 1971
THE MIND OF EVIL (6 episodes)
Writer	*Director*
Don Houghton	Timothy Combe

Regular Cast: see EEE above
Guest stars: see EEE above
Cast: Eric Mason (Green); Roy Purcell (Powes); Raymond Westwell (Governor); Simon Lack (Professor Kettering); Michael Sheard (Dr Summers); Bill Matthews, Barry Wade, Dave Carter, Martin Gordon (Officers); Neil McCarthy (Barnham); Olive Scott (Linwood); Fernanda Marlowe (Bell); Pik-Sen Lim (Ghin-Lee); Kristopher Kum (Fu Peng); Haydn Jones (Vosper); William Marlowe (Mailer); Tommy Duggan (Alcott); David Calderisi (Charlie); Patrick Godfrey (Cosworth); Johnny Barrs (Fuller); Matthew Walters (Prisoner).
Story: The Doctor believes there is an alien Mind Parasite in the Keller Machine, which extracts evil from criminals' minds. In London the Chinese delegate dies at the World Peace Conference. Meanwhile, UNIT is charged with the mission of dumping a banned Thun-

derbolt nerve gas missile at sea. Professor Keller is really the Master, who captures the Doctor and Jo by inciting a riot at Stangmoor Prison. He uses the convicts to hijack the nerve gas missile, which will enable him to destroy the Peace Conference. The Doctor traps the Master by using the Mind Parasite, then explodes it with the nerve gas. But the Master escapes again.

GGG   13 March 1971 to 3 April 1971
THE CLAWS OF AXOS (4 episodes)

Writers   *Director*
Bob Baker,   Michael Ferguson
Dave Martin

Regular cast: see EEE above
Guest stars: see EEE above
Cast: Peter Bathurst (Chinn); Michael Walker, David G. March (Radar Operators); Paul Grist (Bill Filer); Fernanda Marlowe (Corporal Bell); Derek Ware (Pigbin Josh); Donald Hewlett (Sir George Hardiman); David Savile (Winser); Bernard Holley (Axon Man, voice of Axos); Kenneth Benda (Minister); Tim Piggott (Harker); Nick Hobbs (Driver); Royston Farrell (Technician).
Story: An alien spaceship contains the Axons: humanoid, beautiful, and friendly. They ask for hospitality on Earth as their planet has been crippled by a solar flare. But the Doctor is suspicious, and discovers that the Axons, their ship and a substance they brought to Earth called Axonite are all part of a single, collective parasite—Axos—brought by the Master to absorb all living energy on Earth. The Doctor forces Axos into a time loop, exiling it forever in the time vortex.
Book: Doctor Who and the Claws of Axos by Terrance Dicks

HHH   10 April 1971 to 15 May 1971
COLONY IN SPACE (6 episodes)

Writer   *Director*
Malcolm Hulke   Michael Briant
Regular cast: see **EEE** above
Guest stars: Roger Delgado (the Master); Nicholas
Courtney (Brigadier Lethbridge-Stewart).
Cast: Peter Forbes-Robertson, John Baker, Graham
Leaman (Time Lords); John Scott Martin (Robot);
David Webb (Leeson); Sheila Grant (Jane); John Line
(Martin); John Ringham (Ashe); Mitzi Webster (Mrs
Martin); Nicholas Pennell (Winton); Helen Worth
(Mary Ashe); Roy Skelton (Norton); Pat Gorman
(Primitive); Bernard Kay (Caldwell); Morris Perry
(Dent); Tony Caunter (Morgan); John Herrington
(Holden); Stanley McGeach (Allen); Pat Gorman
(Long); Roy Heyman (Alien Priest); John Tardaff
(Leeson); Norman Atkyns (Guardian).
Story: The Time Lords permit the TARDIS to make its
first voyage through Space and Time for more than a
year. The Master has stolen the Doomsday Machine file
and it must be retrieved. The Time Lords despatch the
Doctor and Jo to a bleak Earth-type planet in the year
2471, where they meet the Colonists, farmers who left
Earth because of overcrowding. Since their arrival the
Colonists have faced inexplicable crop failures. There are
two other groups on the planet: the Primitives, the original savage inhabitants, who steal the TARDIS and
imprison Jo in their underground city, and Earthmen
from the Interplanetary Mining Corporation, who have
come to exploit the rich mineral deposits. If successful,
they would make the planet uninhabitable. The IMC
have been demoralising the Colonists with attacks by
robot lizards. An adjudicator from Earth, brought in to
judge between the relative merits of mining and farming,
is impersonated by the Master, whose single aim is to
acquire the Doomsday Machine, guarded in a nearby
ruined city by alien priests. The Doctor and Jo prevent
the exile of the Colonists by exposing the IMC. They also

stop the Master from seizing the Machine by convincing its Guardian—the sole survivor of the race that built the Machine—to set it to self-destruct. The Master escapes.
Book: Doctor Who and the Doomsday Weapon by Malcolm Hulke

JJJ   22 May 1971 to 19 June 1971
THE DAEMONS (5 episodes)

Writer	*Director*
Guy Leopold	Christopher Barry

Regular cast: see EEE above
Guest stars: see EEE above
Cast: Damaris Hayman (Miss Hawthorne); Eric Millyard (Fr Reeves); David Simeon (Alistair Fergus); James Snell (Harry); Robin Wentworth (Professor Horner); Rollo Gamble (Winstanley); Don McKillop (Bert); John Croft (Tom Girton); Christopher Wray (Groom); John Joyce (Garvin); Gerald Taylor (Baker's Man); Stanley Mason (Bok); Alec Linstead (Osgood); John Owens (Thorne); Stephen Thorne (Azal); Matthew Corbett (Jones).
Story: Against the advice of a local white witch, a prehistoric barrow at Devil's End is cut open. A mysterious force erupts, killing the professor responsible for the excavation and concussing the Doctor. When he recovers he finds that the village has been cut off by a heat barrier. The Master—posing as the new vicar—has used psionic science to release the power of a Daemon named Azal. The Daemons are outer-space creatures who came on Earth a long time ago and contributed to the shaping of Human history. Azal, last of the Daemons on Earth, has remained to offer his power to a worthy Human—or to destroy Earth as a flawed experiment! The Doctor shows the Brigadier how to make a tunnel through the heat barrier. The Doctor is attacked by the villagers, under the Master's control, then he meets Azal, who offers him his power. The Doctor refuses and is about to

be destroyed when Jo interposes herself. Azal, confused by this act of self-sacrifice, destroys himself. The Master is finally captured.

Book: Doctor Who and the Daemons by Barry Letts

Ninth Season

Producer
Barry Letts

Script Editor
Terrance Dicks

KKK   1 January 1972 to 22 January 1972
THE DAY OF THE DALEKS (4 episodes)

Writer
Louis Marks

Director
Paul Bernard

Regular cast: Jon Pertwee (the Doctor); Katy Manning (Jo Grant).

Guest stars: Nicholas Courtney (Brigadier Lethbridge-Stewart); John Levene (Sergeant Benton); Richard Franklin (Captain Yates).

Cast: Jean McFarlane (Miss Paget); Wilfrid Carter (Sir Reginald Styles), Tim Condreen (Guerilla); Rick Lester (Ogron); John Scott Martin (Chief Dalek); Oliver Gilbert, Peter Messaline (Dalek voices); Aubrey Woods (Controller); Deborah Brayshaw (Technician); Gypsie Kemp (Radio Operator); Anna Barry (Anat); Jimmy Winston (Shura); Scott Fredericks (Boaz); Valentine Palmer (Monia); Andrew Carr (Guard); Peter Hill (Manager); George Raistrick (Guard); Alex Mackintosh (TV Reporter).

Story: The peace diplomat Sir Reginald Styles is attacked by guerillas, who escape to their 22nd-century world taking the Doctor with them. They are ruled by the Daleks and their ape-like slaves, the Ogrons. The guerillas say they are after Styles because in the 20th century he murdered world leaders, starting a world war which enabled the Daleks to conquer the Earth. They want to prevent this. The Doctor realises that the real murderer, however, was a guerilla sent to kill Styles! The Doctor escapes from the Daleks and hurries back to the 20th century, where he has Styles' house evacuated. The guerilla, Shura, destroys only the Daleks and the Ogrons, who were pursuing the Doctor, with a Dalekanium Bomb. The future is saved.

Book: Doctor Who and the Day of the Daleks by Terrance Dicks

MMM   29 January 1972 to 19 February 1972
THE CURSE OF PELADON (4 episodes)

Writer	*Director*
Brian Hayles	Lennie Mayne

Regular cast: see KKK above

Cast: Henry Gilbert (Torbis); David Troughton (Peladon); Geoffrey Toone (Hepesh); Gordon St Clair (Grun); Nick Hobbs (Aggedor); Stuart Fell (Alpha Centauri); Ysanne Churchman (voice of Alpha Centauri); Murphy Grumbar (Arcturus); Terry Bale (voice of Arcturus); Sonny Caldinez (Sorg); Alan Bennion (Izlyr); George Giles (Captain); Wendy Danvers (Amazonia).

Story: The Time Lords send the Doctor and Jo to the planet Peladon, which has just applied for membership of the Galactic Federation. King Peladon and Chancellor Torbis favour the union; High Priest Hepesh does not. Torbis is murdered and Aggedor, a semi-mythical sacred monster, is blamed. The Doctor arrives and is taken for the Earth's delegate. Other delegates have arrived: Alpha Centauri, Arcturus, and Izlyr of the Ice Warriors. The Doctor finds that Hepesh and Arcturus are behind the murders. With the help of the Ice Warriors the Doctor defeats Arcturus and exposes Hepesh. The Priest orders Aggedor to kill the King but the Doctor has tamed the Monster and it is Hepesh who dies instead. The

Doctor leaves as the true delegate from Earth arrives.
Book: Doctor Who and the Curse of Peladon by Brian Hayles

LLL   26 February 1972 to 1 April 1972
THE SEA DEVILS (6 episodes)
Writer   *Director*
Malcolm Hulke   Michael Briant
Regular cast: see KKK above
Guest star: Roger Delgado (the Master)
Cast: Clive Morton (Trenchard); Royston Tickner (Robbins); Edwin Richfield (Hart); Alec Wallis (Bowman); Neil Seiler (Radio Operator); Terry Walsh (Barclay); Brian Justice (Wilson); Jane Murphy (Jane Blythe); Hugh Futcher (Hickman); Declan Mulholland (Clark); Pat Gorman, Peter Forbes-Robertson (Sea Devils); Eric Mason (Smedly); Donald Sumpter (Ridgeway); Stanley McGeagh (Drew); David Griffin (Mitchell); Christopher Wray (Lovell); Colin Bell (Summers); Brian Vaughn (Watts); Martin Boddey (Walker), Norman Atkyns (Admiral); Rex Rowland (Girton); John Caesar (Myers).
Story: The Doctor and Jo visit the Master, held in captivity on a small island. The Governor, Colonel Trenchard, tells them that ships have been mysteriously disappearing. They investigate and the Doctor is attacked by an underwater Silurian, a man-like lizard called a Sea Devil. The Doctor discovers that the Master, assisted by a misguided Trenchard, is stealing electrical equipment from a naval base to build a machine that will control the Sea Devils—and then enable them to conquer the world. The Doctor enters the Sea Devils' base and tries to encourage peace. But his efforts are frustrated by a depth charge attack ordered by a ruthless politician, Walker. The Doctor persuades Walker to allow him a final attempt at negotiating peace but in the meantime the Sea Devils capture the naval base. The evil Master then forces the Doctor to help finish his machine, which will

73

revive Sea Devil colonies all over the world. The Sea Devils' want to kill the Master, now useless to them, but the Doctor sabotages the machine and escapes with the Master. The Sea Devils are blown up.

Book: Doctor Who and the Sea Devils by Malcolm Hulke

NNN   8 April 1972 to 13 May 1972

THE MUTANTS (6 episodes)

Writers	*Director*
Bob Baker,	Christopher Barry
Dave Martin	

Regular cast: see KKK above

Cast: Paul Whitsun-Jones (Marshal); Geoffrey Palmer (Administrator); Christopher Coll (Stubbs); Rick James (Cotton); James Mellor (Varan); Johnathan Sherwood (Varan's Son); Garrick Magon (Ky); George Pravda (Jaeger); John Hollis (Sondergaard); Sidney Johnson (Old Man); Roy Pearce (Solos Guard); David Arlen (Guard Warrior); John Scott Martin (Mutt); Damon Sanders, Martin Taylor (Guards); Peter Howell (Investigator).

Story: The Time Lords send the Doctor and Jo to the planet Solos to deliver a mysterious message to an unknown party. Solos is about to become independent from Earth, to the chagrin of its sadistic Marshal, whose hobby is to hunt Solonian Mutants. He commissions a Solonian to murder the Earth Administrator and plans to oxygenise Solos's atmosphere. Ky, a Solonian unjustly accused of the murder, takes Jo with him to the planet's surface. The Doctor escapes from the Marshal and tries to find them. On the surface he meets Sondergaard, a doctor who is searching for a cure for the mutating disease which threatens the Solonians. The Doctor, recaptured, is forced to perfect the Marshal's oxygenising machine. Sondergaard gives Ky a crystal which turns him first into a Mutant, then into a super-being. The crystal—found in a cave indicated on the Time Lords' message—enables Ky to kill the Marshal, present his case to the newly arrived Earth Investigator, and help the rest of the Solonians to evolve into super-beings too, part of a century-long evolution process.

Book: Doctor Who and the Mutants by Terrance Dicks

OOO   20 May 1972 to 24 June 1972
THE TIME MONSTER (6 episodes)

Writer   *Director*
Robert Sloman   Paul Bernard

Regular cast: see KKK above
Guest stars: Nicholas Courtney (Brigadier Lethbridge-Stewart); Roger Delgado (the Master); John Levene (Sergeant Benton); Richard Franklin (Captain Yates).
Cast: Wanda Moore (Dr Ingram), Ian Collier (Stuart Hyde); John Wyse (Dr Percival); Terry Walsh (Window-cleaner); Neville Barber (Dr Cook), Barry Ashton (Proctor); Donald Eccles (Krasis); Keith Dalton (Neophite); Aidan Murphy (Hippias); Marc Boyle (Kronos); George Cormack (Dalios); Gregory Powell (Knight); Simon Legree (Sergeant); Dave Carter (Officer); George Lee (Farmworker); Ingrid Pitt (Galleia); Susan Penhaligon (Lakis); Michael Walker (Miseus); Derek Murcott (Crito); Dave Prowse (Minotaur); Melville Jones (Guard); Ingrid Bower (Face of Kronos).
Story: The Master, disguised as Professor Thascales, is working on TOM-TIT—Transmission of Matter through Interstitial Time—a device which would enable him to go through Time to Atlantis and steal the Crystal of Kronos, thus giving him control over Kronos, an entity that lives and feeds on Time itself. The Master fails to control the Kronavore in the 20th century and decides to go back in Time to Atlantis. The Doctor follows him but fails to prevent him from using the Queen of Atlantis to gain access to the Great Crystal. Betrayed by the Queen, the Master unleashes Kronos and orders him to destroy Atlantis. The two Time Lords

fight again in the time vortex. Their two TARDISes collide—but they are saved by a grateful Kronos. The Doctor pleads for the Master and obtains his freedom.

Tenth Season

Producer   *Script Editor*
Barry Letts   Terrance Dicks

RRR   30 December 1972 to 20 January 1973
THE THREE DOCTORS (4 episodes)
Writers   *Director*
Bob Baker,   Lennie Mayne
Dave Martin
Regular cast: Jon Pertwee (the Doctor); Katy Manning (Jo Grant).
Guest stars: William Hartnell (First Doctor); Patrick Troughton (Second Doctor); Nicholas Courtney (Brigadier Lethbridge-Stewart); John Levene (Sergeant Benton).
Cast: Stephen Thorne (Omega); Graham Leaman (Time Lord); Clyde Pollitt (Chancellor); Roy Purcell (President); Laurie Webb (Ollis); Patricia Prior (Mrs Ollis); Rex Robinson (Dr Tyler); Denys Palmer (Palmer).
Story: The energy of the Time Lords is being drained by a black hole. A Cosmic Ray Research Balloon brings back a blob of animated energy which dematerialises things on contact. It expands and besieges the Doctor and Jo in the TARDIS. The only way the Time Lords can help is by sending the Doctor's previous selves. The three Doctors discover the incidents are caused by Omega, a bitter Time Lord trapped behind the black hole in a universe of Anti-matter for thousands of years. Omega wants the Doctor to take his place in his universe

so he can return to ours. But it is too late—Anti-matter radiation has already destroyed the body of Omega, only his will remains and controls his world. Omega wants to destroy the Universe, but the Doctors offer him a positive-matter artefact, thus turning him into a super-nova, whose energy will replenish the Time Lords' reserves. The three Doctors return to their rightful places. The Time Lords lift their exile sentence. The Doctor is free again to roam Time and Space.
Book: Doctor Who—The Three Doctors by Terrance Dicks

PPP   27 January 1973 to 17 February 1973
CARNIVAL OF MONSTERS (4 episodes)
Writer   *Director*
Robert Holmes   Barry Letts
Regular cast: see RRR above
Cast: Stuart Fell (Functionary); Michael Wisher (Kalik); Terence Lodge (Orum); Cheryl Hall (Shirna); Leslie Dwyer (Vorg); Tenniel Evans (Major Daly); Andrew Staines (Captain); Ian Marter (Andrews); Jenny McCracken (Claire); Peter Halliday (Pletrac).
Story: Free to travel in Time and Space again, the Doctor promises Jo a trip to Metebelis 3, the famous blue planet of the Actian Group. But instead he materialises the TARDIS on a cargo ship crossing the Indian Ocean in 1926. Or is it? The Doctor discovers that not only are they on an alien planet trapped in a time loop but they are captives of a showman, Vorg, and his Scope—a miniaturised peepshow of Galaxy life forms. The Doctor tries to escape by entering another section of the Scope—a swamp—where he is confronted by the Drashigs, huge underwater dragons. Finally the Doctor breaks out of the Scope and materialises to full size. He becomes involved in the intrigues of the two natives Kalik and Orum, who plan to overthrow their superior by allowing the Drashigs to escape. Vorg destroys the Drashigs and the Doctor breaks the time link by contriv-

ing to link the TARDIS to the Scope and returning the unwilling participants (Cybermen, Ogrons, etc) to their rightful times and places.
Book: Doctor Who and the Carnival of Monsters by Terrance Dicks

QQQ   24 February 1973 to 31 March 1973
FRONTIER IN SPACE (6 episodes)
Writer   *Director*
Malcolm Hulke   Paul Bernard
Regular cast: see RRR above
Guest star: Roger Delgado (the Master)
Cast: John Rees (Hardy); James Culliford (Stewart); Roy Pattison (Draconian Pirate); Peter Birrel (Draconian Prince); Vera Fusek (President); Michael Hawkins (Williams); Louis Mahoney (Newscaster); Karol Hagar (Secretary); Ray Lonnen (Gardiner); Barry Ashton (Kemp); Lawrence Davidson (Draconian First Secretary); Timothy Craven (Guard); Luan Peters (Sheila); Caroline Hunt (Technician); Madhav Sharma (Patel); Richard Shaw (Cross); Dennis Bowen (Governor); Harold Goldblatt (Professor Dale); Laurence Harrington (Guard); Bill Wilde (Draconian Captain); Stephen Thorne, Michael Kilgarriff, Rick Lester (Ogrons); John Woodnutt (Emperor); Ian Frost (Draconian Messenger); Clifford Elkin (Earth Cruiser Captain); Bill Mitchell (Newcaster); Ramsay Williams (Brook); Stanley Price (Pilot); John Scott Martin (Dalek); Michael Wisher (Dalek voice).
Story: To avoid a head-on collision in Space the Doctor and Jo materialise in the hold of a future Earth spaceship. Almost immediately the ship is attacked. They emerge from the hold and the crew 'see' them as their enemies, the Draconians, an alien humanoid race rivalling Earth for the control of the Galaxy. The Doctor and Jo, however, see the true face of the attackers: Ogrons! A rescue ship takes them all to Earth where they are accused of

being Draconian spies. The Doctor is sent to the Moon but he and Jo are freed by the Master, whose plot is to provoke a space war between Earth and Draconia, using the Ogrons and a hypnotic device. The Doctor escapes and is captured by the Draconians, who believe him to be an *agent provocateur* from Earth. The Doctor succeeds in convincing the Draconians of the truth. Jo is recaptured by the Master and taken to the bleak terrifying Ogron planet. The Doctor follows to rescue her. There he discovers the true masterminds behind the whole plot: the Daleks! The Doctor wins the day but the Master escapes. The Daleks flee after having mortally wounded the Doctor.

Because of the death of Roger Delgado this is the last story to feature the Master until 1976.

Book: Doctor Who and the Space War by Malcolm Hulke
SSS   7 April 1973 to 12 May 1973
PLANET OF THE DALEKS (6 episodes)

Writer	*Director*
Terry Nation	David Maloney

Regular cast: see RRR above
Cast: Bernard Horsfall (Taron), Prentis Hancock (Vaber); Tim Preece (Codal); Roy Skelton (Wester); Jane How (Rebec); Hilary Minster (Marat); Alan Tucker (Latep); Tony Starr (Dalek Supreme); John Scott Martin, Murphy Grumbar, Cy Town (Daleks); Michael Wisher, Roy Skelton (Dalek voices).
Story: Pursuing the Daleks, the Doctor materialises on the planet Spiridon. He has not yet recovered and Jo does not know of his recuperative powers. She sets out alone to find help and meets old allies of the Time Lord, the Thals, who are on a suicide mission to destroy the Daleks. Jo contracts a fungus disease and is cured by a friendly but invisible native. The Thals tell the Doctor that there are thousands of Daleks on Spiridon, immbolised by cold but ready to become an army and conquer the Galaxy with the unwilling help of the Spiridons, who

retain the secret of invisibility. The Doctor finds the whereabouts of the Dalek army and succeeds in reactivating an ice volcano, which refreezes the entire Dalek army.

Book: Doctor Who and the Planet of the Daleks by Terrance Dicks

TTT   19 May 1973 to 23 June 1973
THE GREEN DEATH (6 episodes)
Writer   *Director*
Robert Sloman   Michael Briant
Regular cast: see RRR above
Guest stars: Nicholas Courtney (Brigadier Lethbridge-Stewart); John Levene (Sergeant Benton); Richard Franklin (Captain Yates).
Cast: Stewart Bevan (Professor Clifford Jones); Jerome Willis (Stevens); John Scott Martin (Hughes); Ben Howard (Hinks); Tony Adams (Elgin); Mostyn Evans (Dai Evans); Ray Handy (Milkman); Talfryn Thomas (Dave); Roy Evans (Bert); John Dearth (voice of BOSS); John Rolfe (Fell); Terry Walsh, Billie Horrigan, Brian Justice, Alan Chuntz (Guards); Richard Beale (Minister); Mitzi McKenzie (Nancy); Jean Burgess (Cleaner); Roy Skelton (James).
Story: The villagers of Llanfairfach in Wales are delighted when the local Global Chemicals unit gets a Government grant to build a full-scale refinery. But the project is fiercely opposed by ecologist Professor Clifford Jones. He has set up a commune in the valley and feels the refinery is a threat to his paradise (Nuthutch as the locals call it!). A strange death in some disused mines brings UNIT to the scene. The Doctor, who has managed to get to Metebelis 3 and has found it very hostile, discovers a swarm of giant green maggots and green slime—both fatal to touch—which have come from waste pumped from the refinery. The director, Stevens, refuses to discuss this with UNIT because he has been

taken over by BOSS, the giant computer behind Global Chemicals that has a will of its own. The Doctor uses the only souvenir he brought back from Metebelis 3—a Blue Crystal—to successfully counteract the hypnotic powers of BOSS. He finally succeeds in stopping both the maggots and the maniac computer. Jo Grant falls in love with Professor Jones and leaves UNIT to marry him. The Doctor gives her the Blue Crystal.

Book: Doctor Who and the Green Death by Malcolm Hulke

Eleventh Season

Producer
Barry Letts

Script Editor
Terrance Dicks

UUU   15 December 1973 to 5 January 1974
THE TIME WARRIOR (4 episodes)

Writer
Robert Holmes

Director
Alan Bromly

Regular cast: Jon Pertwee (the Doctor); Elisabeth Sladen (Sarah Jane Smith).

Guest star: Nicholas Courtney (Brigadier Lethbridge-Stewart)

Cast: Kevin Lindsay (Linx); David Daker (Irongron); John J. Carney (Bloodaxe); Sheila Fay (Meg); Donald Pelmear (Professor Rubeish); June Brown (Lady Eleanor); Alan Rowe (Edward of Wessex); Gordon Pitt (Eric); Jeremy Bulloch (Hal); Steve Brunswick (Sentry).

Story: Linx, an alien Captain of the Sontaran race, lands his starship, crippled by the Rutans, in medieval times outside a castle belonging to the robber chief Irongron. Irongron offers shelter in exchange for modern weapons. Linx uses his time machine to reach the 20th century to steal scientists and equipment to repair his starship. The Doctor, accompanied by a stowaway, journalist Sarah Jane Smith, who is investigating the disappearances, uses tracking instruments to find Irongron's castle. The

Doctor is captured and interrogated by Linx, who discovers he is a Time Lord. Despite the resistance of a robot knight built by Linx, Irongron's castle eventually falls. Linx is killed by a local archer and his spaceship blows up.

This is the first time we learn of the name of the Time Lords' planet: Gallifrey.

Book: Doctor Who and the Time Warrior by Terrance Dicks

WWW 12 January 1974 to 16 February 1974
INVASION OF THE DINOSAURS (6 episodes)

Writer	*Director*
Malcolm Hulke	Paddy Russell

Regular cast: see UUU above
Guest stars: see UUU above, and John Levene (Sergeant Benton); Richard Franklin (Captain Yates).
Cast: Noel Johnson (Charles Grover); Peter Miles (Professor Whitaker); Martin Jarvis (Butler); Pat Gorman (UNIT Corporal); James Marcus (Peasant); Ben Aris (Shears); John Caesar (Soldier); Gordon Reid (Phillips); George Bryson (Ogden); Terry Walsh (Looter); John Bennett (General Finch); Martin Taylor (Corporal Norton); Dave Carter (Duffy); Terence Wilton (Mark); Brian Badcoe (Adam); Carmen Silvera (Ruth); Colin Bell (Bryson); Timothy Craven (Robinson).
Story: London is evacuated after prehistoric monsters suddenly appear out of nowhere. The Doctor and Sarah return to find London deserted and under martial law. At first they are arrested as looters but once back with the Brigadier they discover an incredible plot to alter Time. A group of misguided idealists, led by Charles Grover MP, wants to reverse Time, wiping out all Earth's previous history and returning it to a golden age before technological pollution. Captain Yates has been converted to their cause and is working against UNIT. Thanks to his powers as a Time Lord, the Doctor is able to foil the scheme.

Book: Doctor Who and the Invasion of the Dinosaurs by Malcolm Hulke

XXX   23 February 1974 to 16 March 1974
DEATH TO THE DALEKS (4 episodes)
Writer   *Director*
Terry Nation   Michael Briant
Regular cast: see UUU above
Cast: Arnold Yarrow (Bellal); Roy Heymann (Gotal);
Duncan Lamont (Galloway); John Abineri (Railton);
Julian Fox (Hamilton); Joy Harrison (Jill Tarrant); Neil
Seiler (Stewart); Mostyn Evans (High Priest); Terry
Walsh (Spaceman); Steven Ismay (Zombie); John Scott
Martin, Murphy Grumbar, Cy Town (Daleks); Michael
Wisher (Dalek voices).
Story: A space plague attacks all creatures in the Galaxy.
The antidote can only be found on the planet Exxilon,
home of a now savagely hostile and degenerate race. The
Exxilons have rejected all technology since their perfect,
automated City expelled them. The Doctor's TARDIS is
grounded on Exxilon, drained of its power by the City.
The Doctor and Sarah find themselves caught up in a
struggle between Humans, Daleks and Exxilons for pos-
session of the vital antidote. Helped by Bellal, a friendly
Mutant, the Doctor, followed by the Daleks, manages to
get into the City, passes its tests and destroys it. It is
discovered that the Daleks are the cause of the plague.
One of the Humans sacrifices his life to blow up the
Dalek spaceship, saving the precious antidote for
Humanity.
Book: Doctor Who—Death to the Daleks by Terrance
Dicks

YYY   23 March 1974 to 27 April 1974
THE MONSTER OF PELADON (6 episodes)
Writer   *Director*
Brian Hayles   Lennie Mayne

Regular cast: see UUU above

Cast: Ralph Watson (Ettis); Donald Gee (Eckersley); Gerald Taylor (Vega Nexos); Nina Thomas (Queen Thalira); Frank Gatliff (Ortron); Michael Crane (Blor); Stuart Fell (Alpha Centauri); Ysanne Churchman (Voice of Alpha Centauri); Terry Walsh (Captain); Rex Robinson (Gebek); Graeme Eton (Preba); Nick Hobbs (Aggedor); Roy Evans (Rima); Sonny Caldinez (Sskel); Alan Bennion (Azaxyr); Max Faulkner (Miner).

Story: The Doctor returns to Peladon fifty years after his last visit and finds that the spirit of the sacred monster Aggedor is again spreading terror and death. While helping Queen Thalira (King Peladon's daughter), the Doctor finds that some renegade Ice Warriors are behind a plot to seize the mineral wealth of the planet to help an invading enemy—Galaxy 5. The Federation Ambassador, Alpha Centauri, calls upon Federation troops to settle the troubles on Peladon, but the trisilicate mines are occupied by the Ice Warriors and a Human traitor. The Doctor uses the monster-producing machine of his enemies to despatch the Ice Warriors. The traitor is killed by the real Aggedor creature.

Book: Doctor Who and the Monster of Peladon by Terrance Dicks

ZZZ   4 May 1974 to 8 June 1974
PLANET OF THE SPIDERS (6 episodes)

Writer	*Director*
Robert Sloman	Barry Letts

Regular cast: see UUU above

Guest stars: Nicholas Courtney (Brigadier Lethbridge-Stewart); John Levene (Sergeant Benton); Richard Franklin (Captain Yates).

Cast: John Dearth (Lupton); Terence Lodge (Moss); Andrew Staines (Keaver); Christopher Burgess (Barnes); Carl Forgione (Land); Cyril Shaps (Professor Clegg); Kevin Lindsay (Cho-Je); John Kane (Tommy);

Pat Gorman (Soldier); Chubby Oates (Policeman); Terry Walsh (Man with Hat); Michael Pinder (Hopkins); Stuart Fell (Tramp); Ysanne Churchman, Kismet Delgado, Maureen Morris (Spider voices); Ralph Arliss (Tuar); Geoffrey Morris (Sabor); Joanna Monro (Rega); Gareth Hunt (Arak); Jenny Laird (Neska); Walter Randall (Captain); Max Faulkner (Second Captain); Maureen Morris (Great One); George Cormack (K'Anpo).

Story: The Blue Crystal which the Doctor found on the planet Metebelis 3 and gave to Jo Grant as a wedding present is vitally important to the giant spiders who rule the planet. Both Humans and Spiders came to Metebelis 3 in a colonist ship but the local conditions helped the Spiders to dominate the Humans. The Spiders send an emissary to recover the Crystal. The Doctor and Sarah, alerted by the ex-UNIT Captain Yates, are transported to Metebelis 3 and the Doctor leads a revolt of the planet's Human slaves against their Spider rulers. But he finds that meanwhile the Spiders have started their invasion of Earth. The Doctor defeats them again there and returns to Metebelis 3 to confront the Great One—a gigantic mutated spider—with the Crystal of Power. The stone destroys the Spider but the Doctor's body suffers irreparable damage. The Doctor returns to Earth, dying. However, the Tibetan monk Cho-Je, a new incarnation of the Time Lord K'Anpo, accelerates the regeneration process. The Doctor begins to change . . .

Book: Doctor Who and the Planet of the Spiders by Terrance Dicks

Fourth Doctor

Tom Baker
1974–1981

Twelfth Season

Producer
Barry Letts

Script Editor
Robert Holmes

4A   28 December 1974 to 18 January 1975
ROBOT (4 episodes)
Writer   *Director*
Terrance Dicks   Christopher Barry
Regular cast: Tom Baker (the Doctor); Elisabeth Sladen
(Sarah Jane Smith); Ian Marter (Harry Sullivan).
Guest stars: Nicholas Courtney (Brigadier Lethbridge-
Stewart); John Levene (RSM Benton).
Cast: Edward Burnham (Professor Kettlewell); Alec
Linstead (Jellicoe); Patricia Maynard (Miss Winters);
Michael Kilgariff (Robot); John Scott Martin (Guard);
Timothy Craven (Short).
Story: The Doctor is recovering from the effects of his
latest body change. Meanwhile, a giant robot breaks into
a top-secret government establishment and steals the
plans of a new Disintegrator Gun. The Doctor investigates and traces the crimes to a group of dissident scientists known as Think Tank who, led by the formidable
Miss Winters, are planning to take over the world. To do
this they are using a robot designed by Professor Kettlewell, who pretends to oppose them but is really on
their side. The Think Tank steals a Destructor Code
which will enable them to launch a nuclear missile attack

and start the Third World War. UNIT attacks the bunker where they are fortified. In an attempt to protect its masters the robot kills Kettlewell and goes berserk. An infusion of energy provided by the Disintegrator Gun makes it grow to enormous size. The Doctor arrives in time with a metal virus which destroys the robot. Harry Sullivan joins the Doctor and Sarah as they leave in the TARDIS.

Book: Doctor Who and the Giant Robot by Terrance Dicks

Producer
Philip Hinchcliffe

4C   25 January 1975 to 15 February 1975
THE ARK IN SPACE (4 episodes)

Writer	*Director*
Robert Holmes	Rodney Bennett

Regular cast: see 4A above
Cast: Wendy Williams (Vira); Kenton Moore (Noah); Christopher Masters (Libri); John Gregg (Lycett); Richardson Morgan (Rogin); Stuart Fell (Wirrn); Nick Hobbs (Wirrn); Gladys Spencer, Peter Tuddenham (voices).

Story: The TARDIS materialises on a fully automated space station, which appears to be empty and deserted. In reality it contains the whole future population of Earth stored away in deepfreeze until the planet—ravaged by solar flares—is again habitable. Due to a fault in the machinery they have failed to awaken on schedule. The Doctor discovers that the station has been invaded by the Wirrn, giant insect-like creatures, who had laid their eggs in one of the Humans and who plan to take over Earth. They have taken over the body of Noah, leader of the Ark. Expelled from the Ark, Noah sacrifices himself and blows up the Wirrn. The Doctor, Sarah and Harry beam down to Earth to check the planet's condition for the arrival of the Humans from the space station.

Book: Doctor Who and the Ark in Space by Ian Marter

4B   22 February 1975 to 1 March 1975
THE SONTARAN EXPERIMENT (2 episodes)
Writers   *Director*
Bob Baker,   Rodney Bennett
Dave Martin
Regular cast: see 4A above
Cast: Kevin Lindsay (Styre/Marshal); Peter Walshe
(Efrak); Terry Walsh (Zake); Glyn Jones (Krans); Peter
Rutherford (Roth); Donald Douglas (Vural); Brian Ellis
(Prisoner).
Story: On Earth the Doctor discovers that Styre, a Sonta-
ran officer, is conducting cruel experiments on Human
captives—scouts from the old Human colonies sent to
Earth to reclaim it—in order to discover the strength of
Human resistance to a planned invasion of the Galaxy.
The Doctor challenges Styre and defeats him by cutting
him off from his energy sources. Earth is safe for reset-
tlement by the Human race.
Book: Doctor Who and the Sontaran Experiment by Ian
Marter

4E   8 March 1975 to 12 April 1975
GENESIS OF THE DALEKS (6 episodes)
Writer   *Director*
Terry Nation   David Maloney
Regular cast: see 4A above
Cast: Michael Wisher (Davros); John Scott Martin, Max
Faulkner, Keith Ashley, Cy Town (Daleks); Roy Skel-
ton (Dalek voices); Peter Miles (Nyder), Guy Siner
(Ravon), Dennis Chinnery (Gharman); Richard Reeves
(Kaled Leader); John Franklyn-Robbins (Time Lord);
Stephen Yardley (Sevrin); James Garbutt (Ronson);
Drew Wood (Tane); Jeremy Chandler (Gerrill); Pat
Gorman, Hilary Minster, John Gleeson (Thal Soldiers);
Andrew Johns (Kravos); Peter Mantle (Kaled Guard);
Harriet Philpin (Bettan); Max Faulkner (Thal Guard);
Michael Lynch (Thal Politician); Ivor Roberts (Mog-

ren); Tom Georgeson (Kavell).

Story: The Time Lords send the Doctor, Sarah and Harry to the planet Skaro at a time when the war between Thals and Kaleds is reaching its final stage. The Doctor's mission is to prevent the birth of the dreaded Daleks who evolved out of this war. Hunted by both sides in a war-torn world, the Doctor eventually becomes the prisoner of Davros, the brilliant crippled Kaled scientist. Davros has invented a travel machine to house the creature into which the Kaleds, genetically crippled by centuries of warfare, will eventually mutate. But Davros is obsessed by his own creation and is giving it destructive powers and a ruthless intelligence which were not part of the original design. These travel machines are destined to become the Daleks! The Doctor helps to lead a revolt of Kaled scientists, horrified by what Davros is doing. But Davros, in his determination to preserve the Daleks, helps the Thals to destroy his own people with a super-missile. Then he uses the Daleks, now fully operational, first to wipe out the Thal City, then to destroy those remaining Kaleds who oppose him. Some Thals survive. The Doctor manages to entomb Davros in the fortified bunker which has become his final refuge. Here the Daleks turn on Davros, destroying their creator. The Doctor refuses to destroy the Daleks when he has the chance on the grounds that it would be genocide; he says that even from the Daleks a greater good will eventually emerge. Whisked away from Skaro by the Time Lords, the travellers disappear.

Book: Doctor Who and the Genesis of the Daleks by Terrance Dicks

4D   19 April 1975 to 10 May 1975
REVENGE OF THE CYBERMEN (4 episodes)
Writer   *Director*
Gerry Davis   Michael E. Briant
Regular cast: see 4A above

Cast: Alec Wallis (Warner); Ronald Leigh-Hunt (Stevenson); Jeremy Wilkin (Kellman); William Marlowe (Lester); David Collins (Vorus); Michael Wisher (Magrik); Christopher Robbie (Cyberleader); Melville Jones (Cyberman); Kevin Stoney (Tyrum); Brian Grellis (Sheprah).

Story: The Doctor, Sarah and Harry return to the space station only to find that they are in a completely different time period. The station, known as Nerva, is now fulfilling its original function as a space beacon, in orbit around a mysterious planetoid. It is in the grip of a strange plague which has reduced the crew to a mere handful. The Doctor discovers that the plague is carried by Cybermats—deadly machines built by the Cybermen—introduced to the station by a traitor, Kellman. The planetoid is all that is left of Voga, the planet of gold, which was instrumental in the defeat of the Cybermen by the Humans in the Cyberwars centuries ago (gold is deadly to Cybermen). The Vogans have bribed Kellman to attract the remaining Cybermen to Nerva, where they can be blasted out of existence by a Vogan missile, thus freeing the Vogans from a life in hiding. But the Cybermen have other plans. They capture the Doctor and the station crew and, after having attached bombs to them, send them on a deadly errand to the core of Voga. The Doctor eventually helps the Vogans defeat the Cybermen by the use of gold dust. The rest of the machine men are destroyed by the Vogan missile. The Doctor prevents Nerva from crashing down on Voga. The TARDIS arrives and the Doctor finds an SOS from the Brigadier.

Book: Doctor Who and the Revenge of the Cybermen by Terrance Dicks

Thirteenth Season

Producer
Philip Hinchcliffe

Script Editor
Robert Holmes

4F   30 August 1975 to 20 September 1975
TERROR OF THE ZYGONS (4 episodes)

Writer	*Director*
Robert Banks Stewart	Douglas Camfield

Regular cast: Tom Baker (the Doctor); Elisabeth Sladen (Sarah Jane Smith).

Guest stars: Ian Marter (Harry Sullivan); Nicholas Courtney (Brigadier Lethbridge-Stewart); John Levene (RSM Benton).

Cast: John Woodnutt (Duke of Forgill/Broton); Hugh Martin (Munro); Tony Sibbald (Huckle); Angus Lennie (Angus McRannald); Robert Russell (Cabler); Bruce Wightman (Radio Operator); Lillias Walker (Sister Lamont); Bernard G. High (Corporal); Peter Symonds (Soldier); Keith Ashley, Ronald Gough (Zygons).

Story: Summoned back to Earth by the Brigadier, the Doctor investigates a series of mysterious attacks on North Sea oil rigs. Centre of the attacks is the village of Tulloch, very close to Loch Ness. The Doctor discovers that the cause of these attacks is the Loch Ness Monster, in reality a Skarasen, a creature half-animal, half-machine, created by the Zygons, an alien race whose crippled spaceship has rested on the bottom of the Loch for centuries. Unable to return home (their planet was destroyed), the Zygons plan to take over Earth and turn it into a new home planet for their race. Able to change form and take on the physical appearance of Humans, the Zygons have infiltrated the village. The Doctor exposes the Zygons and frees their captives, including the local Duke. The Brigadier blows up the Zygon ship but Broton, leader of the Zygons, now in London, threatens to destroy a World Energy Conference. He is stopped by the Doctor. The Skarasen survives to swim happily back to Loch Ness.

Book: Doctor Who and the Loch Ness Monster by Terrance Dicks

4H   27 September 1975 to 18 October 1975
PLANET OF EVIL (4 episodes)

Writer	Director
Louis Marks	Davis Maloney

Regular cast: see 4F above

Cast: Terence Brook (Braun); Tony McEwan (Baldwin); Frederick Jaeger (Sorenson); Ewen Solon (Vishinsky); Prentis Hancock (Salamar); Michael Wisher (Morelli); Graham Weston (De Haan); Louis Mahoney (Ponti); Haydn Wood (O'Hara); Melvyn Bedford (Reig).

Story: Answering a mayday call, the Doctor and Sarah arrive on Zeta Minor, a planet far out on the edge of the known Universe. A geological expedition from the planet Morestra has run into trouble. Only its leader, Professor Sorenson, is still alive, all the other crew members having been killed by an invisible entity. A military party from Morestra, led by the young Commander Salamar, arrives to investigate. The Doctor and Sarah come under suspicion but when the whole party is attacked by the entity they are released. Zeta Minor is a gate to a universe of Anti-matter, from which the entity originates. They all leave the planet but Sorenson, disregarding the Doctor's advice, has taken some Anti-matter on board. Sorenson turns into an Anti-matter monster and the ship is dragged back to the planet. The Doctor manages to collect all the Anti-matter and captures Sorenson. After the substance is returned to the Anti-matter universe the ship is freed and Sorenson cured.

Book: Doctor Who and the Planet of Evil by Terrance Dicks

4G   25 October 1975 to 15 November 1975
PYRAMIDS OF MARS (4 episodes)

Writer	Director
Stephen Harris	Paddy Russell

Regular cast: see 4F above

Cast: Bernard Archard (Professor Marcus Scarman); Vik

Tablian (Ahmed); Peter Mayock (Namin); Michael Bilton (Collins); Peter Copley (Dr Warlock); Michael Sheard (Laurence Scarman); George Tovey (Ernie Clements); Gabriel Woolf (Sutekh); Nick Burnell, Melvyn Bedford, Kevin Selway (Mummies).

Story: The Doctor and Sarah are returning to UNIT HQ on Earth when the TARDIS is caught up by a mysterious force. Sarah sees an evil face materialise which terrifies her. Egyptologist Marcus Scarman has inadvertently broken into the pyramid prison of Sutekh, last of the Osirians. Sutekh is a creature with god-like powers and his only ambition is to destroy all life in the Cosmos. Defeated by his brother Horus and the other Osirians, Sutekh has lain prisoner for centuries in his pyramid. The Doctor and Sarah arrive in Professor Scarman's house in England (which will later become the site of UNIT's HQ) just as Scarman, possessed by the spirit of Sutekh, returns to build a rocket to go to the Pyramids of Mars; they contain the Eye of Horus, the key to Sutekh's prison. Scarman's robots—dressed as Egyptian mummies—kill Scarman's brother but the Doctor manages, by distracting Sutekh, to blow up the rocket. Sutekh forces the Doctor to take Scarman to Mars in the TARDIS. Scarman destroys the Eye of Horus, but the Doctor returns to Earth in time to prevent Sutekh from leaving the Space/Time tunnel which is the only exit from his prison. Controlling the Time factor of the tunnel, the Doctor sends Sutekh to the ends of Time.

Book: Doctor Who and the Pyramids of Mars by Terrance Dicks

4J   22 November 1975 to 13 December 1975
THE ANDROID INVASION (4 episodes)
Writer   *Director*
Terry Nation   Barry Letts
Regular cast: see 4F above
Guest stars: Ian Marter (Harry Sullivan); John Levene

(RSM Benton).

Cast: Martin Friend (Styggron); Roy Skelton (Chedaki); Max Faulkner (Adams); Peter Welch (Morgan); Milton Johns (Guy Crayford); Stuart Fell (Kraal); Patrick Newell (Faraday); Dave Carter (Grierson); Heather Emmanuel (Tessa); Hugh Lund (Matthews).

Story: The TARDIS lands near what appears to be a peaceful English village. But the inhabitants are strange and unfriendly, responding like robots to mysterious signals. Mechanics with gun-like hands appear from nowhere. The Doctor discovers that they are not on Earth at all but in a replica village built on their own planet by the Kraals, an alien race bent on the conquest of Earth with the aid of Androids. The Doctor and Sarah return to Earth in the Kraal ship in time to foil the Kraal invasion. Some of UNIT's leaders have already been replaced. The Doctor reprogrammes an Android copy of himself to prevent Styggron, the Kraal scientist, from destroying Earth's population with a super-virus.

This is the last UNIT story.

Book: Doctor Who and the Android Invasion by Terrance Dicks

4K   3 January 1976 to 24 January 1976
THE BRAIN OF MORBIUS (4 episodes)

Writer	*Director*
Robin Bland	Christopher Barry

Regular cast: see 4F above

Cast: Philip Madoc (Solon); Colin Fay (Condo); Gilly Brown (Ohica); Cynthia Grenville (Maren); Michael Spice (voice of Morbius); Stuart Fell (Morbius Monster); John Scott Martin (Kriz); Sue Bishop, Janie Kells, Gabrielle Mowbray, Veronica Ridge (Sisters).

Story: The TARDIS lands on Karn, a bleak and stormy planet, where Solon, a disreputable galactic surgeon, is carrying out strange experiments. The planet is also the home of the Sisterhood, witch-like guardians of the mysterious Sacred Flame, from which is prepared the Elixir of Life, an immortality drug shared by the Sisters with the Time Lords. The Flame is dying and the High Priestess, Maren, believes the Doctor is a spy sent by the Time Lords to steal the few precious remaining drops of the Elixir. Meanwhile, the Doctor discovers that Solon is concealing the still-living brain of Morbius, a high-ranking renegade Time Lord and cosmic villain, supposed to have been executed some centuries ago. Solon is making a monstrous new body in which Morbius will live again to lead his followers in the conquest of the Galaxy. The Doctor and Sarah have to battle with Morbius, revived and on the rampage, and with the suspicious Sisterhood. The Doctor defeats Morbius in mental battle, and the body is destroyed by the Sisters, convinced of the Doctor's good faith after he restored the Flame to its former brilliance. Some of the Elixir is used to save the Doctor's life.

Book: Doctor Who and the Brain of Morbius by Terrance Dicks

4L   31 January 1976 to 6 March 1976
THE SEEDS OF DOOM (6 episodes)

Writer	*Director*
Robert Banks Stewart	Douglas Camfield

Regular cast: see 4F above
Cast: Tony Beckley (Harrison Chase); John Challis (Scorby); John Gleeson (Charles Winlett); Michael McStay (Derek Moberley); Hubert Rees (John Stevenson); Kenneth Gilbert (Dunbar); Seymour Green (Hargreaves); Michael Barrington (Sir Colin Thackeray); Mark Jones (Arnold Keeler); Ian Fairbairn (Dr Chester); Alan Chuntz (Chauffeur); Sylvia Coleridge (Amelia Ducat); David Masterman, Harry Fielder (Guards); John Acheson (Major Beresford); Ray Barron (Sergeant Henderson); Mark Jones (Krynoid's voice).
Story: Deep in the permafrost of the Antarctic, scientists

discover two vegetable pods. The Doctor identifies them as Krynoids, an alien species of plant, hostile to all animal life. One of the pods opens and a Krynoid takes over the Antarctic base. In England Harrison Chase, a rich and eccentric botanist, sends two men to steal the remaining pod. They succeed but in the ensuing battle the base and the first Krynoid monster are destroyed. Back in England the second Krynoid quickly develops into a sinister force which threatens to turn the native plants of Earth against Humanity. The Doctor and his allies at the World Ecology Bureau manage to infiltrate Chase's residence, but it is too late to stop the demented millionaire—or the Krynoid. The RAF bombs the Krynoid, now larger than Chase's house, before it germinates.

Book: Doctor Who and the Seeds of Doom by Philip Hinchcliffe

Fourteenth Season

Producer
Philip Hinchcliffe

Script Editor
Robert Holmes

4M   4 September 1976 to 25 September 1976
THE MASQUE OF MANDRAGORA (4 episodes)
Writer
Louis Marks

Director
Rodney Bennett

Regular cast: Tom Baker (the Doctor); Elisabeth Sladen (Sarah Jane Smith)
Cast: Jon Laurimore (Count Frederico); Gareth Armstrong (Giuliano); Tim Pigott-Smith (Marco); Norman Jones (Hieronymus); Antony Carrick (Captain Rossini); Robert James (High Priest); Pat Gorman, James Appleby, John Clamp (Soldiers); Peter Walshe, Jay Niel (Pikemen); Brian Ellis (Brother); Peter Tuddenham

(Mandragora's voice); Peggy Dixon, Jack Edwards, Alistair Fullarton, Michael Reid, Kathy Wolff (Dancers); Stuart Fell (Entertainer).

Story: The TARDIS is drawn off course by the Mandragora Helix, a powerful alien energy complex. Unknown to the Doctor, a portion of Mandragora conceals itself inside the TARDIS, which subsequently lands on Earth. The Doctor and Sarah find themselves in the Dukedom of San Martino in Italy in the 15th century. The evil Count Frederico is planning to usurp the rule of his nephew, Giuliano. He is aided by Hieronymous, the Court Astrologer and secret leader of the Brothers of Demnos, a cult of star-worshippers. Mandragora takes over Hieronymous, seeking to form a bridgehead so that it can kill the great minds of the Renaissance and plunge Earth back into the Dark Ages. Frederico is murdered by Hieronymous now transformed into an energy creature. The Doctor defeats the Helix by draining its energies.

Book: Doctor Who and the Masque of Mandragora by Philip Hinchcliffe

4N   2 October 1976 to 23 October 1976
THE HAND OF FEAR (4 episodes)

Writers	*Director*
Bob Baker,	Lennie Mayne
Dave Martin	

Regular cast: see 4M above

Cast: Roy Pattison (Zazzka); Roy Skelton (Rokon); David Purcell (Abbott); Renu Setna (Intern); Rex Robinson (Dr Carter); Robin Hargrave (Guard); Glyn Houston (Professor Watson); Frances Pidgeon (Miss Jackson); Roy Boyd (Driscoll); John Cannon (Elgin); Judith Paris, Stephen Thorne (Eldrad).

Story: Back on 20th-century Earth Sarah finds a fossilised hand. It is in fact the hand of Eldrad, a Kastrian criminal executed by his own race. Eldrad's hand forces

Sarah to go inside a nuclear research station, where it regenerates itself by absorbing the energy released in an explosion. To save Earth from Eldrad's powers, the Doctor is forced to take him back to Kastria. But in the 150-million-year interval since Eldrad's execution Kastria's civilisation has ended. Eldrad attempts to regenerate his race—but fails because of the measures taken centuries ago by King Rokon as a precaution against Eldrad's possible return. The Doctor and Sarah leave Kastria, abandoning Eldrad to his solitary fate. The Doctor receives a telepathic summons from Gallifrey and—much to her dismay—has to say goodbye to Sarah.
Book: Doctor Who and the Hand of Fear by Terrance Dicks

4P   30 October 1976 to 20 November 1976
THE DEADLY ASSASSIN (4 episodes)
Writer   *Director*
Robert Holmes   David Maloney
Regular cast: Tom Baker (the Doctor)
Cast: Peter Pratt (the Master); Llewellyn Rees (President); Angus Mackay (Cardinal Borusa); Bernard Horsfall (Chancellor Goth); George Pravda (Castellan Spandrell); Derek Seaton (Commander Hildred); Erik Chitty (Coordinator Engin); Hugh Walters (Commentator Runcible); John Dawson, Michael Bilton (Time Lords); Maurice Quick (Gold Usher); Peter Mayock (Solis); Helen Blatch (voice of the Network).
Story: Having seen the assassination of the President of the Council of Time in a vision, the Doctor returns to his home world, Gallifrey. There he is pursued by the Chancellory Guards but manages to avoid capture and breaks into the Panopticon, where he actually watches the President being murdered. The Doctor is arrested and convicted for the murder. To escape execution he proposes himself as candidate for the presidency. Having convinced Castellan Spandrell that he is innocent, the

Doctor discovers that his old enemy the Master is behind the plot. To find out who has been aiding the Master the Doctor has to fight for his life in the fantasy world of the Mind Matrix, where he defeats the real murderer, Chancellor Goth. The Master, whose body has reached the end of his regenerations, seizes the instruments of the presidency to tap the power needed to start a new cycle of lives. But if he releases the power of the Black Hole kept captive under the Panopticon, Gallifrey will be destroyed. The Doctor succeeds in defeating the Master, who escapes, apparently regenerated.

Book: Doctor Who and The Deadly Assassin by Terrance Dicks

4Q   1 January 1977 to 22 January 1977
THE FACE OF EVIL (4 episodes)
Writer   *Director*
Chris Boucher   Pennant Roberts
Regular cast: Tom Baker (the Doctor), and introducing Louise Jameson (Leela).
Cast: Leslie Schofield (Calib); Victor Lucas (Andor); Brendan Price (Tomas); Colin Thomas (Sole); David Garfield (Neeva); Lloyd McGuire (Lugo); Tom Kelly, Brett Forrest (Guards); Leon Eagles (Jabel); Mike Elles (Gentek); Peter Baldock (Acolyte); Tom Baker, Rob Edwards, Pamela Salem, Anthony Frieze, Roy Herrick (voices of Xoanon).
Story: The Doctor lands on a planet where he is captured by a tribe which calls itself the Sevateem. The Doctor survives the Test of the Horda. He discovers that the god Xoanon revered by the Sevateem is a giant computer which has developed a split personality after having been reprogrammed long ago by the Doctor—with his own brain patterns. To correct his mistake the Doctor and a group of warriors from the Sevateem invade the sanctuary of Xoanon and encounter another tribe, the Tesh, who have developed destructive psychic powers. The

Doctor succeeds in removing his brain patterns from Xoanon and in reconciling the two warring tribes. Leela, a Sevateem warrior who befriends the Doctor, slips into the TARDIS and follows the Doctor in pursuit of adventure.

Book: Doctor Who and the Face of Evil by Terrance Dicks

4R   29 January 1977 to 19 February 1977
THE ROBOTS OF DEATH (4 episodes)
Writer   *Director*
Chris Boucher   Michael Briant
Regular cast: see 4Q above
Cast: Russell Hunter (Commander Ulanov); Pamela Salem (Toos); David Bailie (Dask); Rob Edwards (Chub); Brian Croucher (Borg); Tariq Yunus (Cass); David Collins (Poul); Tania Rogers (Zilda); Miles Fothergill (SV7); Gregory de Polnay (D84); Mark Blackwell Baker, John Bleasdale, Mark Cooper, Peter Langtry, Jeremy Ranchev, Richard Seager (Robots of Death).
Story: The Doctor and Leela arrive aboard a huge Sandminer, a mobile factory which mines metal ores from the surface of a deserted planet. The Sandminer has only a token force of Humans, the rest of the crew being robots divided into three classes: Dums, Vocs and Super Vocs. Mysteriously, a member of the crew is murdered and when the Doctor and Leela are discovered they become suspects. Leela discovers that a crew member and a robot are in reality investigators despatched by the company which chartered the Sandminer. There is a sabotage attempt on the ship but the craft is saved by the Doctor. Dask, a member of the crew, is found to be the killer: he is actually Taren Capel, a scientist who has been raised by robots and thinks of them as his brothers. He wants the robots to take control over Mankind and has programmed them to kill. The Doctor, Leela, Commander Ulanov and his aide Toos escape. The Time Lord

releases helium into the atmosphere, changing Dask's voice. The robots, now unable to identify him, destroy him.

Book: Doctor Who and the Robots of Death by Terrance Dicks

4S   26 February 1977 to 2 April 1977
THE TALONS OF WENG-CHIANG (6 episodes)
Writer   *Director*
Robert Holmes   David Maloney
Regular cast: see 4Q above
Cast: John Bennett (Li Hsen Chang); Deep Roy (Mr Sin); Michael Spice (Weng-Chiang/Greel); Trevor Baxter (Professor Litefoot); Christopher Benjamin (Henry Gordon Jago); Tony Then (Lee); Alan Butler (Buller); Chris Cannon (Casey); John Wu (Coolie); Conrad Asquith (PC Quick); David McKail (Sergeant Kyle); Patsy Smart (Ghoul); Judith Lloyd (Teresa); Vaune Craig-Raymond (Cleaning Woman); Penny Lister (Singer); Vincent Wong (Ho).
Story: The TARDIS materialises in Victorian London, where a series of murders are committed by the Chinese Tong of the Black Scorpion, led by Weng-Chiang. Weng-Chiang is in reality Magnus Greel, a war criminal from the future, whose time experiments backfire and whose body needs the energy of others to survive. Victims are provided by Greel's servant, Li Hsen Chang, who performs as magician in a local theatre managed by the boisterous Henry Gordon Jago. The Doctor finds Weng-Chiang's lair in the sewers under the theatre but is chased away by a rat mutated to giant size by Greel. Meanwhile, Li Hsen Chang's men have located the long-lost time cabinet of Weng-Chiang—in the hands of one of the Doctor's friends, Professor Litefoot. Li Hsen Chang fails in his mission to kill the Doctor and recover the Cabinet and is dismissed by Greel. With the help of his Android, Mr Sin, Weng-Chiang recaptures the

cabinet, and the Doctor's friends with it. A dying Li Hsen Chang (he was attacked by Greel's giant rat) gives the address of Weng-Chiang's new refuge to the Doctor. Greel dies a victim of his own life-absorbing equipment and Mr Sin is disconnected by the Doctor.
Book: Doctor Who and the Talons of Weng-Chiang by Terrance Dicks

Fifteenth Season

Producer   *Script Editor*
Graham Williams   Robert Holmes

4V   3 September 1977 to 24 September 1977
HORROR OF FANG ROCK (4 episodes)
Writer   *Director*
Terrance Dicks   Paddy Russell
Regular cast: Tom Baker (the Doctor); Louise Jameson (Leela).
Cast: Colin Douglas (Reuben); John Abbott (Vince); Ralph Watson (Ben); Alan Rowe (Colonel Skinsale); Sean Caffrey (Palmerdale); Annette Woollett (Adelaide); Rio Fanning (Harker).
Story: The TARDIS materialises at the turn of the century on the lone island of Fang Rock. A few hours earlier Vince, the youngest of the three lighthouse-men who are the only inhabitants of the island, watched as a streak of light came down from the sky and landed in the ocean. Not long after, an eerie fog rises and the electrical engineer is mysteriously killed. The Doctor and Leela are suspected of the crime. Meanwhile a passing clipper runs aground. The survivors are rescued and made comfortable. The Doctor tries to convince them to help him against what he now believes to be an alien menace that feeds on electricity. By the time the Doctor realises that

the alien has taken the form of Reuben, the old lighthouse keeper, more members of the small group have died. The alien reveals itself as a Rutan, a blob-like race which is at war with the Sontaran Empire. The Doctor constructs a crude laser and destroys the Rutan and its mother ship.

Book: Doctor Who and the Horror of Fang Rock by Terrance Dicks

4T   1 October 1977 to 22 October 1977
THE INVISIBLE ENEMY (4 episodes)

Writers	*Director*
Bob Baker,	Derrick Goodwin
Dave Martin	

Regular cast: see 4V above, and introducing John Leeson (voice of K9).

Cast: Michael Sheard (Lowe); Frederick Jaeger (Professor Marius); Brian Grellis (Safran); Jay Neill (Silvey); Edmund Pegge (Meeker); Anthony Rowlands (Crewman); John Leeson (Nucleus voice); John Scott Martin (Nucleus Operator); Nell Curran (Nurse); Jim McManus (Opthalmologist); Roderick Smith (Cruickshank); Kenneth Waller (Hedges); Elizabeth Norman (Marius' Nurse); Roy Herrick (Parsons); Pat Gorman (Medic).

Story: A space virus infiltrates an Earth shuttlecraft *en route* to the Titan base. The TARDIS is also attacked by the virus which goes through its flight system and into the Doctor, who is unaware of its presence. When they land on Titan the time travellers are threatened by the shuttlecraft crew. The Doctor discovers that he is carrying the virus nucleus and that incubation tanks are being prepared. He and Leela manage to escape and seek medical assistance at the Bi-Al Foundation, where Professor Marius and his dog-like mobile computer, K9, become their allies. To remove the nucleus from the Doctor's body Marius sends miniaturised clone copies of the Time Lord and Leela into the Doctor's brain. Released and enlarged to Human-size, the nucleus is taken by the possessed crewmen, led by Lowe, who intend to return it to Titan for incubation. To prevent this, the Doctor sets up an explosion which destroys the base.

Book: Doctor Who and The Invisible Enemy by Terrance Dicks

4X   29 October 1977 to 19 November 1977

IMAGE OF THE FENDAHL (4 episodes)

Writer   *Director*

Chris Boucher   George Spenton-Foster

Regular cast: see 4V above

Cast: Wanda Ventham (Thea Ransome/Fendahl Core); Denis Lill (Dr Fendelman); Edward Arthur (Colby); Scott Fredericks (Stael); Edward Evans (Moss); Derek Martin (Mitchell); Daphne Heard (Martha Tyler); Graham Simpson (Hiker); Geoffrey Hinsliff (Jack Tyler).

Story: Dr Fendelman and his assistants, Thea Ransome and Maximilian Stael, through their experiments with a sonic Time Scanner, are in danger of bringing to life the powerful forces that lie dormant in a 12-million-year-old skull. Thea is unware that she is a medium and that through her the Fendahl, an entity which feeds on life itself, will materialise on Earth. Drawn by the Time Scanner, the TARDIS appears nearby and the Doctor attempts to persuade Fendelman of the hazardous nature of his experiments. The Doctor discovers that the Fendahl originated on the Fifth Planet, which was time-looped by the Time Lords. Thea becomes the Fendahl Core and Stael, a practitioner of the black arts, pays for his folly with his life. Using mystical defences the Doctor steals the skull and then uses the Time Scanner to cause a gigantic explosion which destroys the Fendahl. He and Leela take the skull to be jettisoned near a supernova.

Book: Doctor Who and the Image of the Fendahl by Terrance Dicks

4W   26 November 1977 to 17 December 1977

THE SUNMAKERS (4 episodes)

Writer   *Director*
Robert Holmes   Pennant Roberts

Regular cast: see 4T above

Cast: Roy Macready (Cordo); Richard Leech (Gatherer Hade); Jonina Scott (Marn); Michael Keating (Goudry); William Simon (Mandrel); Adrienne Burgess (Veet); Henry Woolf (Collector); David Rowlands (Bisham); Colin McCormack (Commander); Derek Crewe (Synge); Carole Hopkin (Nurse); Tom Kelly (Guard).

Story: The TARDIS lands on Pluto. The Doctor is surprised to find a colony of Humans living there under the light of several small artificial suns. The time-travellers prevent Cordo from committing suicide because of his inability to pay the heavy and unjust taxes requested by the Company, the entity which made the suns around Pluto. Cordo flees the arrival of the Gatherer and leads the Doctor and Leela to the underground city where they meet members of a resistance movement. To convince its hostile leader, Mandrel, that he is not a spy the Doctor attempts to defraud a bank but is captured by the Gatherer, who releases him and places him under surveillance. Joining forces with the rebels the Doctor leads them to capture the PCM production complex where a gas is manufactured and released into the atmosphere to keep the citizens happy. Leela is captured and condemned to be steamed alive. The Doctor saves her. When the PCM gas no longer affects them the citizens rebel and kill the Gatherer. The Doctor confronts the Collector and learns that he is a member of the Usurian race. Unable to deal with the inflation that the Doctor has introduced into his computer, the Usurian shrinks back to its original form and is bottled by the Doctor.

4Y   7 January 1978 to 28 January 1978
UNDERWORLD (4 episodes)

Writers	*Director*
Bob Baker,	Norman Stewart
Dave Martin	

Regular cast: see 4T above

Cast: James Maxwell (Jackson); Alan Lake (Herrick); Imogen Bickford-Smith (Tala); Jonathan Newth (Orfe); Jimmy Gardner (Idmon); Norman Tipton (Idas); Godfrey James (Tarn); James Marcus (Rask); Jay Neill (Klimt); Frank Jarvis (Ankh); Richard Shaw (Lakh); Stacey Tendeter (Naia); Christine Pollon (voice of the Oracle).

Story: At the edge of the universe, where planets are born from cosmic debris, the TARDIS rematerialises on a Minyan ship. To the Minyans Time Lords are gods who helped them build an advanced civilisation. Destroyed by internecine warfare, Minyos is dead; a few Minyans have escaped to found Minyos 2. Jackson and his crew have spent an eternity on the Quest, looking for the long-lost vessel *P7E*, which carried all of Minyos's Race Banks. The Doctor helps Jackson locate the *P7E*, now the core of a planet composed of space debris. The Minyans discover that the *P7E*'s original purpose has been forgotten and that the crew now serve the ship's computer, the Oracle. A hierarchy has formed with the half-man, half-robot Seers tending the Oracle and ruling the Trogs, descendants of the original Minyans. The Doctor and Jackson's crew fight their way to the Oracle's Citadel and manage to steal the two cylinders containing the Race Banks. The Oracle is destroyed by an explosion of its own making. The Minyans blast away, carrying the Trogs to Minyos 2.

Book: Doctor Who and the Underworld by Terrance Dicks

4Z   4 February 1978 to 11 March 1978
THE INVASION OF TIME (6 episodes)

Writer   *Director*
David Agnew   Gerald Blake

Regular cast: see 4T above

Cast: Milton Johns (Kelner); John Arnatt (Borusa); Stan McGowan (Vardan Leader); Chris Tranchell (Andred); Dennis Edward (Gomer); Tom Kelly (Vardan); Reginald Jessup (Savar); Charles Morgan (Gold Usher); Hilary Ryan (Rodan); Max Faulkner (Nesbin); Christopher Christou (Chancery Guard); Michael Harley (Bodyguard); Ray Callaghan (Ablif); Gai Smith (Presta); Michael Mundell (Jasko); Eric Danot (Guard); Derek Deadman (Stor); Stuart Fell (Sontaran).

Story: The Doctor returns to Gallifrey after meeting mysterious aliens in space. Immediately after arriving he demands to see Cardinal Borusa and invokes his right to the presidency. The inauguration plans are monitored by the aliens, identified as Vardans, creatures that have the ability to travel along any wavelength (including thought) and materialise at the end. The Vardans have invaded the Matrix via the Time Lords' own scan beams for watching over the Universe. As President the Doctor exiles Leela from the Capitol because he is afraid the Vardans will be able to read her mind, and tries to neutralise the Vardan threat by finding their planet of origin. In order to do that, however, the Vardans must materialise completely. To gain their trust the Doctor and K9 destroy the transduction barriers that protect Gallifrey. Meanwhile Leela, who has met with the young Time Lady Rodan, encounters the Shobogans, ex-Time Lords now living like savages. They join together to organise a resistance movement. The Vardans finally materialise and the Doctor forces them and their home world into a time loop. As everyone is celebrating a new danger appears: the Sontarans have used the Vardans to gain access to Gallifrey. The Castellan Kelner, who betrayed the Doctor to the Vardans, helps the Sontarans to take control of the Capitol. The Doctor forces Borusa to reveal the location of the Great Key of Time. The Doctor uses the power of the Key to build the supreme weapon, the Demat Gun, which he uses to destroy the Sontarans. In the ensuing explosion the Doctor loses his memory of recent events. Leela chooses to stay on Gallifrey to marry Andred, Captain of the Guards, and K9 stays with its mistress. As the TARDIS heads toward its next destination the Doctor reveals a K9 Mark 2!

Book: Doctor Who and The Invasion of Time by Terrance Dicks

Sixteenth Season

Producer
Graham Williams

Script Editor
Anthony Read

5A   2 September 1978 to 23 September 1978
THE RIBOS OPERATION (4 episodes)
Writer
Robert Holmes

Director
George Spenton-Foster

Regular cast: Tom Baker (the Doctor); Mary Tamm (Lady Romana); John Leeson (voice of K9).

Cast: Iain Cuthbertson (Garron); Nigel Plaskitt (Unstoffe); Paul Seed (Graff Vynda-K); Robert Keegan (Sholakh); Prentis Hancock (Captain); Timothy Bateson (Binro); Ann Tirard (Seeker); Cyril Luckham (White Guardian); Oliver Maguire, John Hamill (Shrieves).

Story: The Doctor is chosen by the White Guardian to assemble the all-powerful Key to Time, which is split into many segments throughout the Cosmos. Joining the Doctor on his quest is a Time Lady, Romanadvoratrelundar (Romana for short) and the new K9 Mark 2. The first stop in the search for the Key's first segment takes them to the winter world of Ribos. Also on Ribos are the two Earth con-men Garron and Unstoffe, out to sell the planet to a deposed tyrant, the Graff Vynda-K.

An important part of their scheme is a lump of Jethrik, one of the most valuable minerals in the Galaxy, which is in reality the first segment of the Key to Time. The Doctor and Romana become involved in Garron's plans, which backfire when the Graff realises he has been cheated. Hunted by the Ribans and by the Graff's men, all seek refuge in catacombs inhabited by ferocious beasts, the Shrievenzales. The Graff calls on a local witch, the Seeker, to locate the Doctor and Garron. In the ensuing hunt the Graff dies in an explosion of his own making. Garron is free to leave Ribos with the Graff's ship, which is full of riches. The Doctor and Romana leave with the first segment.

Book: Doctor Who and the Ribos Operation by Ian Marter

5B   30 September 1978 to 21 October 1978
THE PIRATE PLANET (4 episodes)

Writer	*Director*
Douglas Adams	Pennant Roberts

Regular cast: see 5A above
Cast: Bruce Purchase (Captain); Andrew Robertson (Mr Fibuli); Rosalind Lloyd (Nurse/Queen Xanxia); David Sibley (Pralix); Bernard Finch (Mentiad); Ralph Michael (Balaton); Primi Townsend (Mula); David Warwick (Kimus); Clive Bennett (Citizen); Adam Kurakin (Guard).
Story: The TARDIS heads for the planet Callufrax, where the second segment of the Key is located, but instead lands on Zanak. Zanak is a hollow world equipped with massive transmat engines which enable it to jump through the space vortex and rematerialise around another world, draining it of its matter and energy. Romana is captured by guards and taken to the Bridge to the Captain, half-man, half-machine, but the Doctor rescues her. He realises that the planet is in the process of absorbing Callufrax. The Time Lords find unusual allies in the Mentiads, a race of telepaths who have recently

appeared on Zanak. The Doctor organises an attack on the Bridge but is captured. He finds that the true master of Zanak is not the Captain but its original ruler, Queen Xanxia, who has been using the pillaged energies to keep her original body alive. The Doctor and the Mentiads try to stop the planet's next jump through the space vortex, which would take Zanak to Earth. During the fighting the Captain attempts to revolt and is killed by Xanxia. Cut off from her much needed energy sources, Xanxia is shot by a rebel. The Doctor discovers that Callufrax, now reduced to a football-sized husk, is the second segment of the Key to Time. The Time Lords leave after the citizens of Zanak have destroyed the Bridge.

5C   28 October 1978 to 18 November 1978
THE STONES OF BLOOD (4 episodes)
Writer   *Director*
David Fisher   Darrol Blake
Regular cast: see 5A above
Cast: Susan Engel (Vivien Fay); Beatrix Lehmann (Professor Rumford); Nicholas McArdle (De Vries); Elaine Ives-Cameron (Martha); Gerald Cross, David McAlister (Megara voices); James Murray, Shirin Taylor (Campers).
Story: The TARDIS rematerialises on Earth. The Doctor and Romana follow the trace of the third segment of the Key to Time to an ancient Druidic circle where they meet Professor Amelia Rumford and her friend Vivien Fay. The Doctor suspects he might find a clue as to the location of the segment from the local Druidic priest—but he is nearly sacrificed to a pagan goddess, the Cailleach. Rescued by Professor Rumford, the Doctor finds that the priest has been killed by the Ogri, stone creatures that feed on blood. The Ogri serve the Cailleach and normally look like part of the stone circle. The Doctor finds that the Cailleach is in reality Vivien Fay, who has been living on Earth for about 3,000 years.

Before he can alert Romana, Vivien Fay, using some of the properties of the third segment of the Key, sends her to a spaceship orbiting in hyperspace above the circle. The Doctor manages to follow and by accident frees the Megara, justice machines sent with the ship to judge an alien criminal, Cessair of Diplos. The Megara threaten to execute the Doctor but the Time Lords trick them into probing the mind of Vivien Fay. When they realise that she is in fact Cessair the justice machines turn her into a stone megalith. The Doctor manages to capture the third segment (Vivien's necklace) and banishes the Megara.

This story was the 100th *Doctor Who* story.

Book: Doctor Who and the Stones of Blood by Terrance Dicks

5D   25 November 1978 to 16 December 1978

THE ANDROIDS OF TARA (4 episodes)

Writer	*Director*
David Fisher	Michael Hayes

Regular cast: see 5A above

Cast: Peter Jeffrey (Count Grendel); Neville Jason (Prince Reynart); Simon Lack (Zadek); Paul Lavers (Farrah); Lois Baxter (Madame Lamia); Declan Mulholland (Till); Martin Matthews (Kurster); Cyril Shaps (Archimandrite).

Story: The Doctor and Romana land on Tara, a peaceful planet where science is the domain of the commoners while the rulers enjoy a life patterned after chivalristic models. The Doctor decides to take a fishing holiday and sends Romana looking for the fourth segment of the Key to Time—which she locates in the shape of a local statue. The Time Lady is captured by the evil Count Grendel who takes her to be an Android of Princess Strella, her exact double, whom he keeps prisoner in the hope that eventually by marrying her he will become King of Tara. Meanwhile, the Doctor is approached by the rightful pretendant to the Taran throne, Prince Reynart, who asks him to repair his Android double, which he plans to use to avoid assassination during the coronation ceremony. Reynart is kidnapped by Grendel and the Doctor uses the Android in his place, foiling the plans of the Count. Grendel attempts to kill the Doctor, who succeeds in freeing Romana. The Count manages to destroy Reynart's Android and recaptures Romana. He now plans to marry Reynart to the Time Lady (posing as the captive Princess Strella), and then kill Reynart and marry Romana. The Doctor arrives in time to rescue the Prince and defeat the Count.

Book: Doctor Who and the Androids of Tara by Terrance Dicks

5E   23 December 1978 to 13 January 1979
THE POWER OF KROLL (4 episodes)
Writer   *Director*
Robert Holmes   Norman Stewart
Regular cast: see 5A above
Cast: Neil McCarthy (Thawn); Philip Madoc (Fenner); Grahame Mallard (Harg); Glyn Owen (Rohm-Dutt); John Leeson (Dugeen); Terry Walsh (Mensch); Carl Rigg (Varlik); John Abineri (Ranquin); Frank Jarvis (Skart).
Story: The Doctor and Romana land on Delta Magna's third moon, which is mostly swamps and marshes. They are caught up in a feud between the Swampies and a group of Human technicians. The Swampies are green humanoids, original descendants of the Delta Magnans who were given the moon as a sort of reservation by the Human colonists of Delta Magna. They resent the intrusion of the technicians, who have set up a plant to collect methane from the swamps and convert it into protein, to be shipped by rocket back to Delta Magna. Romana is captured by the Swampies and the Doctor by the refinery people. Both are highly suspicious of the newcomers and the Swampies offer Romana as a sacrifice to their god Kroll. The Doctor rescues her and they escape, along

with Rohm-Dutt, a gun smuggler. They discover that he has been paid by Thawn, the refinery Controller, to give the Swampies non-functional guns, thus justifying his extermination policies. Rohm-Dutt is killed by Kroll, a squid-like creature of titanic size. The monster attacks the refinery. Thawn plans to blast the creature with a rocket, thus threatening the entire population of the moon. He is stopped by Varlik, a native who has now realised that Kroll is not a god. The Doctor finds that Kroll's gigantic size was caused by his swallowing a holy relic of the Swampies—the fifth segment of the Key to Time—and removes it, thus causing the monster to be split into many smaller entities.

Book: Doctor Who and the Power of Kroll by Terrance Dicks

5F   20 January 1979 to 24 February 1979
THE ARMAGEDDON FACTOR (6 episodes)

Writers	*Director*
Bob Baker,	Michael Hayes
Dave Martin	

Regular cast: see 5A above
Cast: Lalla Ward (Princess Astra); John Woodvine (Marshal); William Squire (The Shadow); Ian Saynor (Merak); Davyd Harries (Shapp); Valentine Dyall (Black Guardian); Barry Jackson (Drax); Ian Liston (Hero); Susan Skipper (Heroine); John Cannon, Harry Fielder (Guards); Iain Armstrong (Technician); Pat Gorman (Pilot); Stephen Calcutt (Super Mute).
Story: The search for the final segment to the Key to Time takes the Doctor, Romana and K9 to the twin planets of Atrios and Zeos. A full-scale nuclear war is raging between the twin worlds. The Marshal, who commands the Atrian defence, is intent on pursuing the war to its ultimate conclusion. The Doctor suspects that the Marshal is being controlled from elsewhere. The final segment of the Key seems to have some connection with

113

the Atrian Royal Princess, Astra, who has been kidnapped by the evil Shadow, a servant of the Black Guardian. The Doctor, Romana and K9 go in search of her and find themselves trapped on Zeos, a planet that appears deserted but for Mentalis, a giant computer which has been waging the war on Atrios. Lured on by the Shadow, the Marshal threatens a final assault on Zeos, ignorant of the fact that this will trigger Mentalis to destroy itself and both planets. To stop the oncoming armageddon the Doctor is forced to use the incomplete Key to time-loop the Marshal. The Doctor goes to the lair of the Shadow, a third planet in orbit between Zeos and Atrios, where his friends are now under the control of the Shadow. He manages to ally himself with Drax, an itinerant Time Lord and the builder of Mentalis. The Doctor discovers that the last segment of the Key is Princess Astra herself, who ceases to exist as she completes the Key. The Time Lords manage to recapture the Key and escape with it. Mentalis is disconnected by Drax and the Marshal's nuclear attack is directed by the Doctor to the Shadow's planet, which is destroyed. The Doctor now faces the Black Guardian himself, disguised as the White Guardian. Deciding that the Key is too powerful for anyone to hold, the Doctor splits it and scatters it again throughout the Cosmos, thus restoring the Princess to her original form. To escape the wrath of the Black Guardian, the Doctor equips the TARDIS with a randomiser.

The first episode of this story marks the 500th episode of *Doctor Who*.

Book: Doctor Who and the Armageddon Factor by Terrance Dicks

Seventeenth Season

Producer
Graham Williams

Script Editor
Douglas Adams

5J   1 September 1979 to 22 September 1979

DESTINY OF THE DALEKS (4 episodes)

Writer	*Director*
Terry Nation	Ken Grieve

Regular cast: Tom Baker (the Doctor); Lalla Ward (Romana)

Cast: Tim Barlow (Tyssan); Peter Straker (Commander Sharrel); Suzanne Danielle (Agella); Tony Osoba (Lan); David Gooderson (Davros); Roy Skelton (Dalek voices); Cy Town, Mike Mungarvan (Daleks); Penny Casdagli (Jall); David Yip (Veldan); Cassandra (Movellan Guard).

Story: Romana's body regenerates and she adopts the likeness of Princess Astra of Atrios. The two Time Lords land on a desolate planet. They are intrigued by evidence of drilling operations deep underground. While investigating, the Doctor is trapped in a collapsed building and is rescued by the Movellans, a race of beautiful humanoids led by Commander Sharrel. The Doctor discovers that he is once again on Skaro, home planet of the Daleks. Meanwhile, Romana has been captured by the Daleks and put to work with the other enslaved Humans working on Skaro for some unknown purpose of the Daleks. An escaped prisoner, Tyssan, leads the Doctor and the Movellans underground, where the Doctor finds Romana, who has escaped the Daleks by pretending to be dead. They discover what the Daleks were seeking all the time: Davros. They take him prisoner and return to the Movellan ship. The Movellans turn out to be a merciless, logical, robotic race which has been fighting the Daleks for centuries, but a stalemate has been reached. The Daleks need Davros to gain an advantage and the Movellans plan to use the Doctor. With the help of Tyssan the Doctor prevents the Movellans from destroying Skaro and succeeds in defeating the Daleks. The two Time Lords leave and Tyssan takes Davros prisoner back to Earth.

Book: Doctor Who and the Destiny of the Daleks by Terrance Dicks

5H   29 September 1979 to 20 October 1979
CITY OF DEATH (4 episodes)
Writer   *Director*
David Agnew   Michael Hayes
Regular cast: see 5J above
Cast: Julian Glover (Scaroth/Count Scarlioni/Captain Tancredi); Catherine Schell (Countess Scarlioni); Tom Chadbon (Duggan); David Graham (Professor Kerensky); Kevin Flood (Hermann); Peter Halliday (Soldier); Pamela Stirling (Louvre Guide); John Cleese, Eleanor Bron (Art-lovers).
Story: A crippled Jagaroth spaceship piloted by Scaroth explodes on takeoff in 400 million BC on Earth. In 1979, Paris, the Doctor and Romana meet a British detective named Duggan. They uncover a plan by Count and Countess Scarlioni to steal the Mona Lisa with the aid of alien technology. The Count is selling a collection of art treasures to finance his time travel experiments, conducted by Professor Kerensky. In a room in the Count's castle which has been sealed for centuries the Doctor discovers six more apparently genuine Mona Lisas. He goes back to Renaissance Italy to find Leonardo da Vinci. There, the Time Lord is taken prisoner by Captain Tancredi, who looks exactly like the Count. Tancredi is forcing the Master to produce more Mona Lisas. The Doctor discovers that the original explosion split Scaroth into 12 segments scattered at different periods of Human history. The alien has influenced Mankind's scientific evolution so that his 20th-century self can go back in time to prevent the explosion. The Doctor returns to the 20th century to find Romana and Duggan prisoners of the Count. Scaroth, now revealed as a green scaly creature with one red eye, kills Kerensky and the Countess and embarks on his journey back through time. The Doctor

and his friends follow in the TARDIS. The Doctor
realises that it is the explosion of the Jagaroth ship which
will create life on Earth. The Doctor tries in vain to
reason with Scaroth. Duggan prevents the alien from
succeeding by knocking him unconscious. Dragged back
through time, Scaroth perishes in the explosion of his
machines.

5G   27 October 1979 to 17 November 1979
THE CREATURE FROM THE PIT (4 episodes)
Writer   *Director*
David Fisher   Christopher Barry
Regular cast: see 5J above, and David Brierley (voice of K9).
Cast: Myra Frances (Lady Adrasta); Eileen Way
(Karela); Geoffrey Bayldon (Organon); David Telfer
(Huntsman); John Bryans (Torvin); Edward Kelsey
(Edu); Tim Munro (Ainu); Tommy Wright (Guard Mas-
ter); Terry Walsh (Doran); Morris Barry (Tollund);
Philip Denyer, Dave Redgrave (Guards).
Story: The Doctor and Romana arrive on Chloris, an
abundantly fertile world which is extremely short of
metal. They fall into the hands of the Lady Adrasta, a
ruler whose power derives from her monopoly of metal
on the planet. She polices her people with carnivorous
Wolf Weeds controlled by her Huntsman. Those who
displease her, she throws into the Pit, a worked-out mine
which contains a terrifying creature. The Doctor finds
himself in the Pit with Adrasta's Court Astrologer,
Organon. There, he discovers that the creature is in
reality an ambassador from Tythonus, who came to
Chloris to exchange metal—which the Tythonians have
in abundance—for chlorophyll, which is extremely rare
on Tythonus. Frightened of losing her monopoly,
Adrasta has kept Erato, the ambassador, imprisoned in the
Pit for many years. Erato has not been able to communi-
cate with the Chlorians but with the Doctor's help, he is
eventually able to reveal the truth. The Huntsman turns

117

against Adrasta and she is killed by Erato. Adrasta's treatment of the Tythonian envoy almost brings total disaster to Chloris even after her death, but with Erato's help the Doctor manages to save the planet and the ambassador returns to Tythonus.

Book: Doctor Who and the Creature from the Pit by David Fisher

5K   24 November 1979 to 15 December 1979
NIGHTMARE OF EDEN (4 episodes)

Writer	*Director*
Bob Baker	Alan Bromly

Regular cast: see 5G above
Cast: David Daker (Rigg); Lewis Fiander (Tryst); Jennifer Lonsdale (Della); Geoffrey Bateman (Dymond); Barry Andrews (Stott); Stephen Jenn (Secker); Geoffrey Hinsliff (Fisk); Peter Craze (Costa); Pamela Ruddock (Computer voice); Richard Barnes, Sebastian Stride, Eden Phillips (Crewmen); Annette Peters, Lionel Sansy, Peter Roberts, Maggie Peterson (Passengers).

Story: Two spacecraft, the luxury liner *Empress* and the *Hecate*, crash into one another while one is semi-dematerialised and ready to jump into hyperspace, with the result that they become fused. Among the passengers of the *Empress* is Tryst, a naturalist, and his assistant, Della. They have with them a Continuous Event Transmuter, a machine which allows whole areas of land to be removed from planets and to be stored on laser crystals, along with the local fauna, which continue to exist and develop while on the crystal recording. As a result of the crash, the CET becomes unstable and releases hordes of Mandrels, monsters from the planet Eden, onto the *Empress*. The Doctor also discovers that someone on board is smuggling Vraxoin, one of the most dangerous addictive drugs in the Universe, which incapacitated the *Empress* navigator (hence the crash). Suspected of being the smugglers, the Doctor and Romana are pursued by

118

the *Empress* crew. The Time Lord discovers that the real smuggler is Tryst, and that Vraxoin is made from the very essence of the Mandrels. Tryst and the pilot of the *Hecate* are planning to beam the contents of the Eden crystal to the planet Azure below. The Doctor succeeds in separating the two ships and in preventing the smugglers from carrying out their plans. After Tryst's capture by customs agents the Doctor returns the Mandrels and the Eden sample to Eden.
Book: Doctor Who and the Nightmare of Eden by Terrance Dicks

5L   22 December 1979 to 12 January 1980
THE HORNS OF NIMON (4 episodes)
Writer   *Director*
Anthony Read   Kenny McBain
Regular cast: see 5G above
Cast: Simon Gipps-Kent (Seth); Janet Ellis (Teka); Graham Crowden (Soldeed); Michael Osborne (Sorak); Malcolm Terris (Co-pilot); Bob Horney (Pilot); Clifford Norgate (Nimon voice); John Bailey (Sezom); Robin Sherringham, Bob Appleby, Trevor St John Hacker (Nimons).
Story: The TARDIS, whilst immobilised for repairs, falls into a gravity whirlpool along with a damaged ship taking a group of young men and women from the planet Aneth to the planet Skonnos, where they are to be presented as tribute to the Nimon, a mysterious entity who lives at the centre of a huge labyrinthine complex. The Nimon has promised to return Skonnos to its former glory if the Skonnons supply young men and women and radioactive hymetusite crystals—which they have in turn exacted from the peaceful planet Aneth. The Doctor repairs the Skonnon ship but is left behind in his inoperative TARDIS by the treacherous co-pilot who flies to Skonnos, taking Romana with him. Soldeed, leader of Skonnos and servant of the Nimon, sends the

Anethan sacrifices, Romana and the co-pilot into the Nimon complex. The Doctor, who has managed to repair the TARDIS, arrives on Skonnos and follows them. Inside the complex they find the Nimon, a bull-headed alien who kills the co-pilot. The Doctor discovers that the Nimon is preparing to bring the rest of his race to Skonnos through a black hole in Space fed by the hymetusite crystals. The Nimons are like a galactic plague of locusts, jumping from planet to planet after having drained them of their resources. One of them is sent ahead to promise wealth and power to unsuspecting races, and builds the huge complex which enables the rest of the Nimons to infiltrate and eventually take over the host planet. At the other end of the space tunnel Romana finds a dying planet, Crinoth. With the help of Seth, a young Anethian, the Time Lord succeeds in destroying the complex, leaving the Nimons stranded on Crinoth, where they perish. Thanks to K9, the Doctor and his friends finally escape from the complex, which is destroyed.

Book: Doctor Who and the Horns of Nimon by Terrance Dicks

5M

SHADA (6 episodes)

This story was not broadcast because filming was interrupted by a strike at the BBC.

Writer	*Director*
Douglas Adams	Pennant Roberts

Regular cast: see 5G above

Cast: Denis Carey (Professor Chronotis); Daniel Hill (Chris Parsons); Victoria Burgoyne (Clare Keightley); Christopher Neame (Skagra); Gerald Campion (Porter); Derek Pollitt (Caldera); John Hallett (Constable); David Strong (Passenger); Shirley Dixon (Ship); James Coombes (voice of Krargs).

Story: In a remote space station called Think Tank a

scientist called Skagra steals the minds of his colleagues, and escapes. Meanwhile, the Doctor and Romana visit present-day Cambridge to see Professor Chronotis, a retired Time Lord living incognito as a don. He wants them to take a book, *The Ancient Law of Gallifrey*, back to the planet of the Time Lords. Unfortunately it has accidentally been taken away by a post-graduate student, Chris Parsons. He and a colleague, Clare Keightley, are mystified by the book, which is made of no earthly substance. Skagra arrives on Earth in search of the book because it will give him directions to the Time Lord prison planet of Shada, where he believes Salyavin, the most powerful Time Lord, is imprisoned. Skagra needs access to Salyavin to learn from him the secret of projecting a print of his own mind into every sentient being in the Universe, a technique which will guarantee the success of his plan for galactic domination. The Doctor retrieves the book but Skagra sends his mind-sapping Sphere after the Doctor. On a bicycle chase through the streets of Cambridge the Doctor loses the book, which is found by Skagra. Skagra heads for Shada in the TARDIS, having captured Romana to operate it. The Doctor takes Skagra's own spaceship and with K9 and Chris Parsons goes to Think Tank in search of Skagra and Romana. He encounters the monstrous crystalline Krargs, Skagra's servants. It transpires that Chronotis's rooms in Cambridge are the inside of his own TARDIS, which he uses to rescue the Doctor from the Krargs. Against the Professor's wishes and with the aim of rescuing Romana the Doctor follows Skagra to Shada, where Skagra has freed the criminals, including a Dalek, a Cyberman and a Zygon—but Salyavin is not there. Professor Chronotis turns out to be Salyavin. The Doctor wins a mind battle with Skagra and imprisons him in his own spaceship. Returning to Earth, the Doctor leaves the Professor in Cambridge, promising to keep his identity secret.

Eighteenth Season

Producer
John Nathan-Turner

Script Editor
Christopher H. Bidmead

5N   30 August 1980 to 20 September 1980
THE LEISURE HIVE (4 episodes)
Writer
David Fisher

Director
Lovett Bickford

Regular cast: Tom Baker (the Doctor); Lalla Ward (Romana); John Leeson (voice of K9).
Cast: Adrienne Corri (Mena); David Haig (Pangol); Laurence Payne (Morix); John Collin (Brock); Nigel Lambert (Hardin); Martin Fisk (Vargos); David Allister (Stimson); Ian Talbot (Klout); Andrew Lane (Chief Foamasi); Roy Montague (Argolin Guide); Harriet Reynolds (Tannoy voice); Clifford Norgate (Generator voice).
Story: The Doctor and Romana visit the Leisure Hive on the planet Argolis, an artificial environment which is an entertainment centre for galactic travellers. The Argolins themselves are a race dying from the consequences of a war with their old enemies, the reptilian Foamasi. Accidents mysteriously happen at the Tachyon Recreation Generator—the pride of the Hive—and the Argolin leader, Mena, is pressurised by her Earth agent, Brock, to sell the Hive to the Foamasi, an offer which is violently opposed by her son, Pangol. Mena believes she can be rejuvenated by Earth scientist Hardin's Tachyon experiments, but the man is a fraud. The two Time Lords are arrested on suspicion of having murdered Hardin's assistant, who discovered that the Foamasi had secretly invaded the Hive. While experimenting with Hardin's machine, the Doctor ages considerably. With Mena dying, Pangol—who is revealed as a creation of the TGR—takes over the Hive and attempts to duplicate

himself into an army to war against the Foamasi. Instead, a rejuvenated army of Doctors leave the machine. The Foamasi invaders reveal themselves as agents of their government and unmask Foamasi saboteurs who had been impersonating Brock and his lawyer, Klout. The randomised Doctors disappear and Mena and Pangol are turned into younger versions of themselves by the TGR.

5Q 27 September 1980 to 18 October 1980
MEGLOS (4 episodes)

Writers	*Director*
John Flanagan,	Terence Dudley
Andrew McCulloch	

Regular cast: see 5N above
Cast: Edward Underdown (Zastor); Jacqueline Hill (Lexa); Crawford Logan (Deedrix); Colette Gleeson (Caris); Bill Fraser (Grugger); Frederick Treves (Brotadac); Simon Shaw (Tigellan Guard); Christopher Owen (Earthling).

Story: Zastor, leader of the planet Tigella, has sent for the Doctor because the Dodecahedron—the crystal which powers their underground civilisation—is failing. Meanwhile, on the nearby dead planet of Zolfa-Thura, a band of Gaztak space raiders meet the cactus-like Meglos, who secures their help for his plan to steal the Dodecahedron. For that purpose, Meglos assumes the appearance of the Doctor, whom he imprisons in a Chronic Hysteresis. Having escaped, and arriving on Tigella, the Doctor is blamed for the theft and condemned by the crystal worshippers to be crushed to death. Meglos is unmasked by Caris, one of the Tigellans who believe that their planet's surface should be reclaimed from the aggressive vegetation that overruns it. Meglos is inadvertently freed by Romana after she escapes from the Gaztaks, who have captured her. The Doctor freed, the Time Lords rush to Zolfa-Thura where Meglos intends to release the power of the Dodecahedron. The Doctor now impersonates Meglos and mis-sets the crystal, which explodes, destroying the last Zolfa-Thuran and the Gaztaks. Without its power, the Tigellans are forced to begin the reclamation of their planet.

5R   25 October 1980 to 15 November 1980
FULL CIRCLE (4 episodes)

Writer	*Director*
Andrew Smith	Peter Grimwade

Regular cast: see 5N above, and introducing Matthew Waterhouse (Adric).

Cast: Richard Willis (Varsh); Bernard Padden (Tylos); June Page (Keara); James Bree (Nefred); Alan Rowe (Garif); Leonard Maguire (Draith); George Baker (Login); Tony Calvin (Dexeter); Norman Bacon (Marsh Child); Andrew Forbes (Omril); Adrian Gibbs (Rysik); Barney Lawrence (Marshman).

Story: The TARDIS goes through a Charged Vacuum Emboitement and the two Time Lords find themselves on planet Alzarius in E-Space. There, they encounter a community of Humans, descendants of a starliner which crashed 40 centuries earlier. The community is ruled by the Deciders who have preserved the ship and hope eventually to leave the planet with it. They warn the community of the incoming Mistfall, a time when mysterious creatures rise up from the marshes. A group of youths, called Outlers, led by Varsh and his brother Adric, refuse to believe them. However, the myth proves to be real and marsh creatures start appearing. Romana becomes their victim but is rescued by the Doctor. With the help of Adric the Time Lord discovers that the starliner people are actually evolved marshmen who have taken over and ritually maintained the ship. The Doctor enables them to pursue their destiny by leaving Alzarius, and Adric stows away in the departing TARDIS.

5P   22 November 1980 to 13 December 1980

STATE OF DECAY (4 episodes)
Writer   *Director*
Terrance Dicks   Peter Moffatt
Regular cast: see 5R above
Cast: William Lindsay (Zargo); Rachel Davies (Camilla); Emrys James (Aukon); Iain Rattrary (Habris); Thane Bettany (Tarak); Arthur Hewlett (Kalmar); Stacy Davies (Veros); Clinton Greyn (Ivo); Rhoda Lewis (Marta); Dean Allen (Karl); Stuart Blake (Zoldaz); Stuart Fell (Roga); Alan Chuntz (Guard).
Story: The TARDIS lands on a medieval-like planet ruled tyranically by King Zargo and Queen Camilla. The Doctor and Romana are captured by rebels led by the technologically minded Kalmar. Having convinced the rebels that they are on their side, the Time Lords discover that the King and the Queen are the original officers of an explorer ship which left Earth a thousand years earlier. Meanwhile, Adric who has been hiding among the peasants is captured by the King's Councillor, Aukon. The Time Lords discover that the Tower—Zargo's castle—is in reality the lost spaceship, and that the King, the Queen and Aukon are vampires! The entity that drew them into E-Space and turned them into vampires, the Great Vampire (last survivor of a race destroyed by the Time Lords), lies in the ground beneath the Tower, ready to rise. The Doctor arranges a concerted attack on the Tower and uses one of the scout ships as a stake to kill the Great Vampire. Zargo, Camilla and Aukon crumble into dust.

5S   3 January 1981 to 24 January 1981
WARRIORS' GATE (4 episodes)
Writer   *Director*
Steve Gallagher   Paul Joyce
Regular cast: see 5R above
Cast: Clifford Rose (Rorvik); Kenneth Cope (Packard); David Weston (Biroc); Jeremy Gittins (Lazlo); Freddie

Earlle (Aldo); Harry Waters (Royce); David Kincaid (Lane); Vincent Pickering (Sagan); Robert Vowles (Gundan).

Story: The TARDIS is hijacked by Biroc, a Time-sensitive Tharil, who has just escaped from the privateer ship of Captain Rorvik. Biroc steers the TARDIS into an eerie misty void and leaves. The Doctor follows him to find a mirror-like gateway guarded by axe-wielding robots, the Gundans. Romana falls prisoner of Rorvik, who arrives at the gateway just as the Doctor manages to pass through to the other side of the mirror. There, the Time Lord finds Biroc and learns that the Tharils, once rulers of a vast empire and notorious slave-owners, were captured by the Gundans, which were made by their rebellious slaves. The Tharils are now kept prisoner in the impervious dwarf star alloy hold of Rorvik's ship. Meanwhile, on the other side of the gateway, Romana has been freed by another Tharil, Lazlo. Rorvik is now determined to blast his way out of the void. The back-blast of the ship shatters the hull and releases the Tharils. They return to E-Space with Romana and K9 while the Doctor and Adric are blown back into N-Space.

5T   31 January 1981 to 21 February 1981
THE KEEPER OF TRAKEN (4 episodes)
Writer   *Director*
Johnny Byrne   John Black
Regular cast: Tom Baker (the Doctor); Matthew Water-house (Adric); and introducing Sarah Sutton (Nyssa).
Cast: Anthony Ainley (Tremas); Sheila Ruskin (Kassia); Denis Carey (the Keeper); John Woodnutt (Seron); Margot Van De Burgh (Katura); Robin Soans (Luvic); Roland Oliver (Neman); Geoffrey Beevers (Melkur); Liam Prendergast, Philip Bloomfield (Fosters).
Story: The Union of Traken is a place of universal harmony held together by the bioelectronic Source, which is controlled by the Keeper. The current Keeper's mil-

lenium is about to end and he asks the Doctor and Adric for their help. Meanwhile, on Traken, Consul Kassia marries Consul Tremas and finds to her distress that the Keeper has chosen Tremas as his successor. A calcified, evil creature called Melkur seizes upon this fault to manipulate Kassia to have her husband imprisoned, along with the Doctor and Adric, on false charges. As Melkur becomes the new Keeper of Traken, he reveals himself to be the Master! Thanks to an almost catastrophic diversion, during which Adric and Nyssa—Tremas's daughter—nearly succeed in destroying the Source, the Doctor manages to defeat his old enemy. In a last minute twist the Master seizes upon Tremas's body to effect his thirteenth regeneration.

5V   28 February 1981 to 21 March 1981
LOGOPOLIS (4 episodes)
Writer   *Director*
Christopher H. Bidmead   Peter Grimwade
Regular cast: see 5T above, and introducing Janet Fielding (Tegan Jovanka) and Peter Davison (the Doctor).
Cast: Anthony Ainley (the Master); John Fraser (Monitor); Dolore Whiteman (Aunt Vanessa); Tom Georgeson (Detective Inspector); Christopher Hurst (Security Guard).
Story: The Doctor decides to repair the TARDIS's chameleon circuit and goes to England to find a real police box, thereby falling into a complex dimensional trap devised by the Master. A young air hostess, whose aunt is later murdered by the renegade Time Lord, enters the TARDIS thinking it to be a police box. The Doctor, having been warned by the mysterious Watcher that an enormous trial lies ahead, rushes to Logopolis, a city inhabited by pure mathematicians. There, the Monitor, who is in charge of Logopolis, reveals a copy of the famous Pharos Computer Project on Earth. The Master, who has been interfering with the City in his

plans to destroy the Doctor, accidentally causes it to stop functioning. The Monitor reveals that the Universe has passed the point of normal heat death and that its life has been extended only by his people's calculations. Realising the consequences of the Master's actions—the dissolution of the Universe—the two Time Lords team up and together they go to the Pharos Project on Earth, to beam the Logopolitan Program into deep Space. The Master now plans to blackmail the Cosmos into submission, and the two Time Lords begin a fight which causes the Doctor to fall to his death. The Master escapes while the Doctor's body regenerates.